THE GOD OF ELISHA

Elijah Mwashayenyi

Published in Great Britain by
L.R. Price Publications Ltd, 2019
27 Old Gloucester Street,
London, WC1N 3AX
www.lrpricepublications.com

Cover artwork by L.R. Price Publications Ltd
Copyright © 2019
Used under exclusive and unlimited licence by
L.R. Price Publications Ltd.

Elijah Mwashayenyi Copyright © 2020

The right of Elijah Mwashayenyi to be identified as author of this work has been asserted in accordance with sections 77 and 78 of the Copyright, Designs and Patents Act, 1988.

ISBN-13: 9781838061050

DEDICATION

For my wife Mirriam and first born Kuda, who endured so much during my ten months absence while I was in Japan.

THE GOD OF ELISHA

ELIJAH MWASHAYENYI

Table of Contents

Chapter One: A Deadly Encounter –

Page 1

Chapter Two: The Bushwhackers –

Page 20

Chapter Three: George of the Ambulance –

Page 36

Chapter Four: The Praying Mantis –

Page 48

Chapter Five: Valley of the Shadow of Death –

Page 64

Chapter Six: The Swing of Death -

Page 78

Chapter Seven: The God of Elisha –

Page 89

Chapter Eight: The Man Who Came Back from the Cold -

Page 103

Chapter Nine: Love is in the Air –

Page 122

Chapter Ten: The Final Twists -

Page 135

THE GOD OF ELISHA

When man and deadly reptile go on a collision course, the fate of the former looks sealed; the medical professionals look baffled by a seemingly impossible case. A whole host of characters find themselves tangled in the nightmare of a total stranger, including a twelve-year-old bushwhacker who has the steely resolve of a grown man, a beautiful nurse with unshaken faith and a fiery preacher who has the audacity to call upon his God.

A moving story of faith, love and the hand of God working miracles in people's lives.

CHAPTER ONE

A Deadly Encounter

The black mamba slithered forward, its movements as silent and as deadly as those of a predator out to inflict a fatal blow on its prey. The prey, which was some fifty or so metres away, was a brown squirrel perched on a rock and which appeared to be nibbling at something. The snake did not know it then, but it was a nut the rodent had found nearby. The rock presented a very nice sitting position and a good place for eating. However, this was not the squirrel's usual place for eating. Some two hundred metres to the south of the rock was a hole in an old and dying tree which had been home to the squirrel and its family for more than a year. Today the furry little creature was so hungry that, when it miraculously stumbled on a nut, it decided to consume it as close to the spot of its discovery as possible. The actual consumption was not very hasty, despite the gnawing hunger. As usual, the nibbling was fast while it lasted but was frequently punctuated by lapses in between the nibbles, as if the animal was savouring its food or was listening for any kind of threat from nearby. As soon as it finished its nut, the squirrel would be on its way home.

For a brief moment, it wondered whether its female counterpart had found something too. It quickly forgot about this and decided to enjoy its meal in the “safe” place.

“Safe” was the exact opposite of the situation creeping up on the squirrel. What it did not realize was that it had crossed paths with an equally hungry black mamba and was now in one of the most dangerous positions in which it had ever been. The reptile had also had a long barren day. Worse still, it had gone for quite a while without food. The dead and the dying animals in its drought-stricken environment were too large for it to swallow. Birds and rodents were not dying just yet. Now its fortunes seemed to be about to change with the sighting of the squirrel. For a moment or two, the mamba paused, putting attack plans into place. This was one prey it meant to get and so everything had to be done to perfection.

Being the largest, most venomous snake in the wild, the black mamba lay almost four metres long. Though relatively slender, it still presented the image of a large snake. Its coffin-shaped head looked deceptively small, but the eyes were something one would not want to see even in a nightmare, let alone real life. They were dark and lifeless and yet very much alive, with the sort of death message in them that would cause goosebumps even on a combat soldier. Like all black mambas, "black" did not describe the skin colour. It described the mouth. Black mambas are usually brown or grey in colour, the colour tending to darken with age. This one was dark grey, but there was no way you could mistake it for black unless in poor light or if you had a vision condition. The scales on its skin made it even more menacing. They were oblique, smooth and satiny and became smaller and smaller as they reached its long tapering tail.

The big snake went into attack mode. It slithered as silently as it could towards the rock and squirrel, ignoring the hot ground as its eyes and mind focused on the task at hand. The mamba was used to this kind of thing. Like all other mambas, it hunted by day and so had mastered the technique of getting very close to its prey with little chance of being detected. The squirrel still appeared to be cautious but it did not see or hear the predator. So the Mamba came on. Now, it was twenty metres out. These last few metres were going to be very difficult to cover without detection. The vegetation was even sparser than within the distance it had already covered in this particular hunt. Yet there were still two things in the snake's favour. The skin colour easily blended with the landscape and the squirrel was almost facing away from the snake, so that the reptile was approaching its prey from roughly its blind side. These were two advantages the mamba intended to exploit fully. If it failed, the night would be very long. It did not want to think about failure.

The mamba knew a few discouraging things about squirrels, though. Generally, they were alert animals and were arguably the most difficult to surprise. Quite often, the surprise was on the predator's side. Unfortunately for any predator, once a squirrel detected danger, it would wag its tail excitedly and chatter away so loudly that the whole neighbourhood would know that something was up. Any predator in this predicament would quickly realize the futility of its pursuit and take its hunt elsewhere.

Still, the black mamba had made quite a few squirrel kills during its lifetime. Some of them had been very difficult, yet it knew that this one would be the most difficult of them all. Something at the back of the snake's mind kept telling it that the squirrel would not remain a sitting duck for too long. Sooner or later, the nut would disappear, with possible disappointing results for the snake.

So the long black mamba slithered on, its head held low, as if it meant to burrow into the ground. Now it was pausing after every metre or so to check its progress. It had covered a lot of ground, but it was still outside striking range. A few minutes later it got into striking range and stopped. The big snake started to raise its head to strike the fatal bow. The fate of its prey was sealed. During the next few seconds the meal would be on the table. It was a hunt that would have shattered all the snake's records had it been sealed, but it wasn't. Fate was to rear its ugly head, according to the snake, and change the course of events.

At the precise moment that the black mamba started to raise its head, the squirrel appeared to have been startled by something. It suddenly dropped what remained of the nut and sprinted away to safety before the reptile could do anything. The mamba was sure that it had not been detected. That meant something else must have intruded. The mamba knew that there was no way it would get its prey now, so something else had to be settled. Keeping its head just above the rock, its eyes surveyed the surroundings looking for something to vent its anger on.

It did not take long to see its new victim. It was a human being, walking right up to the rock where the squirrel had been sitting a few seconds earlier. The mamba completely disappeared behind the rock, knowing full well that it should have seen the intruder earlier. But that was now water under the bridge. The present had to be dealt with in the best way the snake knew how. So the snake lowered its head behind the rock and waited, ready to strike. This time it was not going to be for food, but for revenge.

***

A lone skinny herd boy stood on an anthill staring at the sun that was bound to set within the next two hours. His thin frame, silhouetted against the background of a pitiless sky, presented the image of despair. You could see the lost hope on his face. He had every reason to be this way.

As people say: when the Pacific sneezes, Africa catches a cold. During the previous summer, the Pacific seemed to have sneezed. El Niño also appeared to have responded. The result was that the Intertropical Convergence Zone that normally brought summer rain to southern Africa had stayed north, refusing to shift to the south. The impact was devastating; the worst drought in living memory. Now the drought was entering its second summer. Today there was no sign of clouds in the sky, not even the Cirrus or Altocumulus. In fact, the boy did not remember the last time he had seen a cloud in the sky. No clouds, no rain, nothing but the burning sun; the sky was about as empty as a football pitch during the off-season.

It was not just the weather that had seen better days. The cropping season had not even kicked off. The once-green pastures were no more. Some people were still hoping against hope that the tide would turn. They kept their concerned faces turning towards the sky every day as if begging for mercy. Come to think of it, maybe they were. All the same, the sky did not smile back. The irony of it all was that meteorologists were still prophesying worse times to come.

The boy looked at the sky for the thousandth time that day and then looked at his animals. His despair did not get any better. His once-large herd of cattle had dwindled to five animals; two skinny cows, a dying calf and two donkeys he had left at home. Grass and water for animals were getting scarcer and scarcer every day. All they had had that day were a few mouthfuls of wilted leaves from branches the boy had broken from nearby mopani trees and some muddy water from puddles nearby. Once upon a time, the puddles had been part of a big river. That was now history. The leaves and water would not last long now. The remaining cattle would go the same way. The boy knew this very well and, like everybody else, could do nothing about it.

A few minutes earlier, the boy had waved to a game warden. He looked as if he was inspecting the game fence. Although he was too far away to recognize this particular warden, he still liked him. In fact, he liked all game wardens. Once in a while they gave his people game meat. They also took care of rogue elephants and stray lions. Not that he was scared of these animals. He was young all right, but he was not scared of them or of any other animal for that matter. He was a bushwhacker and so he knew how to survive in the wild. Only he did not like to see crops destroyed by elephants or his animals killed by marauding lions.

Now, as he stood there, his bow and arrow in one hand, a long whip in the other and a quiver secured on his back, he made up his mind that, in a few minutes, he would be heading home, a kilometre or so away. Not that he was enthusiastic about getting home. On one hand he wanted to go and rest. On the other he did not like the idea of going to a home where there was scarcely anything to eat. There was one source of comfort, though. Food or no food, it was home and there was no place better than home. Yet he could not get it out of his mind that the last decent meal his family had had was when drought relief food was delivered by government officials a month before. During that particular week his community had been lucky. Ten buffaloes had been culled by game staff and the meat distributed in his village. Maybe he should have asked the game warden he had seen earlier about the next culling exercise, he thought for a moment. He was not the sort of person to cry over spilt milk and so he quickly pushed the thought out of his mind.

The boy started to climb down the anthill. As he made the effort to get the third step, something caught his ears that made him freeze in his tracks.

***

Warden John Sithole inspected the damaged game fence and quickly resolved that it would have to be repaired soon. He studied the ground around the fence and reached another conclusion. A rogue elephant had decided that life in the game reserve had become too monotonous for its liking and so opted to venture outside. Perhaps it had gone in search of food. All the same, the exercise had not been a gentle one, hence the extensive damage on the fence. Maybe he should have gone back and talked to the boy he had seen earlier, he thought, but quickly pushed the idea out of his mind. Sooner or later, someone was bound to make a report. An elephant was too big an animal to roam anywhere unnoticed. At least there were no crops and hence the stray animal was less likely to go on rampage.

He stood there for several minutes, estimating how much the repairs would cost. Warden Sithole was tall, being just over six feet, with the slim build of an athlete that looked good on him. His twenty-seven-year-old face was light in complexion, handsome and always carried a smile even when there was nothing to smile about. It was the kind of face anyone would like at first sight.

As he continued with his bush trip, John passed a gemsbok and a kudu that looked as if they had had better days. The kudu looked as if it was digging a root or something. This was understandable. With the grass being so dry fresh animal food was at a premium. He took out his camera from the bag and took a few photos. The animals did not seem to be frightened of him. Maybe they were used to seeing game wardens and tourists or maybe they did not have the energy to run away. After taking the photographs he put his camera back into its bag and walked on.

John was a great lover of wildlife. Having graduated from the University of Zimbabwe with an Honours Degree in Zoology, five years earlier, he had joined the Department of National Parks and Wildlife soon afterwards. He was stationed in Gonarezhou Game Reserve, some fifty kilometres south-east of the town of Chiredzi in the south-east Lowveld of Zimbabwe. Although he was based at the game reserve's biggest camp, Chipinda Pools Camp, he liked camping out, carrying out studies and doing errands. This time he had camped out for three days almost ten kilometres south of Chipinda with his team. It was a very difficult time to camp out, but John seemed oblivious to the Lowveld heat.

Earlier in the afternoon, John had decided to leave his team and scout the south of their temporary camp. He holstered his revolver, picked up his water bottle and camera case and drove south along a track which seemed to have been last used years before. The track continued to wind, remaining about a kilometre from the game fence. It eventually came to a dead end. John checked his bearings and continued with his scouting on foot walking towards the fence.

During the whole afternoon the game warden did not like what he saw. It was not an unfamiliar sight but each time he saw the carnage he wished the good old rainy days would come back soon. It would be the understatement of the year to say that animals were dying. They were being annihilated. The last estimates that had come up a week earlier had shown that the dead included some four thousand impala, two thousand buffaloes and two thousand elephants, which were anything up to a third of the population of these species. John kept praying that the drought would break soon, otherwise if the current situation continued for a few more months, there would be no game reserve to talk about. That did not augur well for his job security and that of his colleagues.

Talking about praying, John remembered that he and two of his team-mates would have to get back to Chipinda

Pools for their Wednesday evening prayer meeting. They would come back to the temporary camp the next morning. He did not feel like travelling at night that day. Not that he hated travelling at night. In fact, he loved it, especially when there was a full moon. It was romantic……..What was he thinking about? he asked himself. What did he know about the subject? He let his feelings run away with him for several minutes. Yes, one of these days he would meet his life partner. He really looked forward to getting married. He had no one in his life at the moment. Twice he had thought he had met a life partner. Twice he was wrong.

The first time he was in college. There was a lady who fascinated him. She was in the Christian Union just like him. She liked him and he liked her, and it looked as if they were falling madly in love. Their colleagues seemed to think so as well. When it turned out that the lady in question was just using the Christian Union as a cover for her real social life, John had second thoughts. The inevitable affair, which never was, died a natural death and everyone lived happily ever after. Well, not quite. John felt a bit sad at the turn of events. For a long time, he blamed himself for being blind. He eventually got over it and he turned to what he did best – studying. As it was his final year in college and exams were only a few months away, he simply immersed himself in books and gave them his best shot. He obtained a first-class degree.

As a matter of fact, the lady also watched the dying of a relationship which she knew was imminent. It was just a matter of time before John popped the three-word phrase. She could see it in his eyes. Then as suddenly as it had started, the association withered and died. She did not have to be told that her real character had been unearthed. She knew that sooner or later he would come to know about her. She hoped it would be later rather than sooner. She was not the kind of person who took prisoners. When the time came, she would count her costs and move on. Men were like buses. She missed one, she got another. It was just too bad if one had a weak heart. She would break it and it was entirely up to him to get it fixed. Unfortunately, the time had come prematurely in John's case. She disappeared from the Christian Union for good. John never discovered what new hunting ground she had moved to. He did not care and so he never ventured to find out.

His second encounter with a prospective life partner was also abortive but it turned out to less tragic than the first. Actually, both of them settled for second best. Two years after joining the Department of National Parks and Wildlife, a new game warden came to Gonarezhou Game Reserve to join him and his colleagues. She was a nice lady in all respects. She was also a person who feared God. Before John and Constance realized it, they were best friends. They were still the best of friends up to now and they also made a good working combination. Neither of them had tried to venture into anything beyond friendship. They respected each other for what they were and appeared quite content with that.

With all these thoughts and more, John found himself at the game fence. He walked for about three kilometres southward along the fence before he discovered the damaged portion. After the inspection he continued south for another kilometre or so, found no further damage and decided to walk straight towards his jeep. Once he completed this lap of his scouting he would have walked in a right-angled triangle with the third lap of the journey being the hypotenuse. If he kept a good pace, he would get to the vehicle in good time to drive and reach the temporary camp before sunset.

He walked for almost a kilometre without incident. Then, quite suddenly, his eyes caught something which fascinated him. A squirrel was perched on a rock, a good sixty metres or so away. It appeared to be nibbling at something and it did not seem to have noticed him. This surprised him a little. John knew a lot about squirrels. They were clever little creatures which could sense danger from afar. He liked them because they warned him and his colleagues when there was a snake or some other potentially dangerous creature nearby. He smiled to himself as his mind made a decision. He would get as close as possible to the squirrel and photograph the little thing.

He trod very carefully, using tree cover as much as possible as he made his advance. He stopped behind a baobab tree and retrieved his camera from its case. He was still some forty metres out. He would have to get closer to get a good picture. He advanced again and came to stop behind a mopani tree. It was not a very thick tree and it was all he could do to stay behind it and remain undetected. The squirrel was now less than thirty metres away. He was sure this was as close as he would get before the squirrel saw him and sprinted away. He would have to employ the zooming button of his camera.

John partially emerged from behind the tree, his camera ready for action and focused on the little creature which was almost facing his direction. He pressed the zoom switch of his camera and smiled. He was a bit far all right, but it could have been worse. He liked the way the squirrel handled what was apparently a nut. He wished he had brought a video camera. A video was a good visual aid when it came to lectures in addition to being an important part of his personal collection. He held his breath and pushed the red button on his camera. Two things happened at the same time. The camera clicked, taking the picture of the squirrel, not in its perched position but in a slightly different one. At the precise moment that the camera started to click, the squirrel dropped its nut and sprinted away to safety, chattering excitedly. John was sure that the squirrel had not been startled by the click of the camera. The sound was very low, and the events had occurred so simultaneously that there was only one explanation. He had been spotted.

John put his camera back in its case and walked up to the rock where the squirrel had been sitting less than a minute earlier. On arrival he picked up what remained of the nut the rodent had been eating and examined it. There was less than a quarter remaining. It was a pity that the little creature had not finished its meal, he said to himself. In this drought, the nut must have meant a lot to the animal. Maybe the squirrel would come back and finish it once he was gone. But then, maybe it would not. Some other hungry creature might come across it before the squirrel returned.

An unmistakable hiss made him freeze right there in front of the rock. He was still holding the nut in his left hand. Though he did not know it then, John had made a mistake when he got to the rock. He never looked to see what lay behind the rock. He had no reason to. After all, the squirrel had been sitting on that rock. He had not seen anything else through his camera either. It is not quite clear what would have happened had John checked behind the rock. Maybe he would have slightly altered the course of events that followed. As the situation stood, the course of events looked destined in one way. His fate was sealed.

In confrontation, many snakes usually try by all means to intimidate the enemy by raising their heads as high as possible, with hissing, sometimes spitting and flickering of the tongue. The cobra will spread its hood. That usually makes it really menacing, even when the snake is small. The black mamba is one of those snakes that do not really need to intimidate an enemy. It is deadly enough as it is and the worst part of it is that it knows it. Still, it will go through the ritual. This snake can stand on less than a third of its body length, making it very tall. Its hood is not anything to write home about, but it does not make it any less menacing.

John saw the black mamba rise from behind the rock with what must have been more than half of its length. The hood was there all right and the enormous mouth was wide open, revealing the black interior. The long fangs looked as deadly as they were meant to. The flickering tongue told him that the reptile meant business. John knew a lot about snakes and about black mambas in particular. The latter was the most respected reptile in wildlife circles. He knew that the snake which was before him needed very little provocation to give him the kiss of death. So he stood very still, not even flinching. That only lasted a few seconds.

What the warden did not realize was that the black mamba needed no further provocation in order to strike. The snake was as angry and as dangerous as it could ever be. In the blink of an eye, John watched in horror as the largest, most venomous snake of the wild started to swing at him. In that split-second, John knew that he was a dead man.

CHAPTER TWO

The Bushwhackers

In the second that the black mamba started to strike, something at the back of John's mind told him to make a move. The warden had been in tight spots before but maybe only one seemed to parallel this situation, maybe. He had been called to make quick draws all right, but the principle of his job was to shoot as a last resort. Last resorts did not come any closer than the current crisis. So, as the coffin-shaped mamba's head started to fly at him, his right hand flew at his holster while the left arm went up to try to block the snake from striking his head. It was the fastest draw John had ever made; one that would have made John Wayne, the legendary American cowboy, green with envy. There was a blur as the hand went for the gun, the weapon cleared leather and came up spitting fire. Yet, even then, John knew he was too late. Worse still, he missed. Shooting at a moving target is difficult enough. Shooting a striking black mamba takes something close to a miracle, even at point blank range. Miracles were not happening just yet.

Even as the gun roared, the snake was already striking its victim's left arm. As is its custom, the reptile had meant to strike the head but when it saw two new moving targets, it changed its mind with its head in full flight and struck the nearest, the left arm. John felt a searing pain as the deadly fangs found their mark and the equally deadly poison entered his bloodstream. He could not help it but instinctively dropped his gun. He held his bitten arm as the reptile's head went back to its ready position. The snake continued to sway dangerously, mouth still open, the black interior, long fangs and quivering forked tongue adding to the unmistakable threat display. John knew that the black mamba usually struck once and would be quite content with that if there was no need for a second strike. He also knew that if he made any further sudden move, that could be interpreted as a provocation, a second strike would be guaranteed and possibly a third.

So man and reptile stood there on either side of the rock, the latter daring the former to make a move. Blood mixed with some poison started to drip from the two fang marks on his arm. John did not even look at this. Although he knew that his lifeline was draining away, he dared not take his eyes off the vicious snake. He did not have fancy ideas about his fate. He knew that his bushwhacker days had come to an end. He was sure that as the poison took effect, a number of very painful things would happen to him.

He would be lucky to survive the next few hours. The young man thought about many things as he contemplated his tragic fate. He was not really scared of dying. It was the pain he would have to go through that he was not prepared to face. There was also another dimension to this. There was so much he still needed to achieve in both his professional and social life. If only he had not dropped his gun. If only the snake would go away. Yet, even the chances of survival were still close to nil given the distance to his jeep or even the communal homes. So he remained where he was facing the snake, like someone waiting for a miracle to happen.

Indeed, miracles do happen. Before both man and reptile realized what was happening, the situation took a new twist as, a few minutes into the stand-off, a third creature entered the equation.

***

Warden Constance Bitu paced up and down outside her tent, her thoughts playing havoc in her head. If it was not dusk any person nearby might have noticed the disturbed frown on her face. Notwithstanding the time of day, it was apparent that the movements were those of a worried person. Her dilemma was this: Warden John Sithole should have arrived by sunset. He was driving the jeep they would use to get to Chipinda Pools for the evening's prayer meeting. Worse still, John was the main speaker tonight and she was scheduled to chair the meeting. Without John, Constance and Assistant Warden Michael Chiponda were grounded. Their colleagues at Chipinda would be worried and confused. There was one thing that bothered Constance and it was probably the thing that bothered her the most. If there was one person who was always on schedule, it was John. If he said he would be there at dawn, come hell come high water, he would be there at dawn. Everyone in his outfit respected him for being a man of his word. It was not like John to just disappear with no phone call or even a radio message. Although she was trying to reject it, Constance had a feeling that something had gone horribly wrong. Her thoughts went back to the only time John had been late. That was a year earlier. When he eventually turned up, he had a harrowing story to tell. John had stumbled on a wounded lioness. Worse still, it had two cubs. Without any warning, the queen of the jungle had gone into attack mode. John did not want to turn the little cubs into orphans but at most he had two or three seconds to make up his mind. Two hours later when he arrived at their camp site, he had two orphans in his hands.

"Hi there," a voice from almost behind her shook her out of her reverie.

"Hello Mike, still no sign of John," she responded. It was not a question.

"I wonder what has delayed him."

"I have been wondering that myself. It is unlike John to be late."

"Yeah, I know. I think the word 'late' does not exist in his vocabulary."

"He's one of a kind." The admiration in Constance's voice was unmistakable.

"Any speculation on what might have happened?"

"I have been trying hard not to. His cell phone is out of reach and he is not answering the radio. I don't have a good feeling about this. He could have had a breakdown or something… I wish those hand radios would be back soon. John needs one. Perhaps he's on his way on foot."

"Within half an hour or so, the folks at Chipinda will be starting to worry. We should contact them to tell them that we will be late."

"You are right, but there is nothing else we can do for now except to wait. Maybe he has run into a situation that needs divine intervention. Let's do something about it." So the two bushwhackers started praying out there in the open. Constance did not realize how close to the truth she was then. If both of them knew the course of events that had been triggered two hours earlier, they might have started an all-night vigil.

***

The twelve-year-old was sure it was a gunshot. Judging from the direction of the sound he was also certain that the warden had something to do with it. That could only mean one thing. He must have shot some animal. Chances were that it was something he could get meat from. With this in mind, the boy did not hesitate to go into action.

Forgetting about his cattle, he dropped his whip by the anthill and ran due east towards the game fence. His estimates were that he would reach his destination in a few minutes. Then he would help with whatever needed to be done, including skinning the animal and cutting it up. His parents would be very happy if he brought home some meat. The idea gave him renewed strength. Soon he flashed past the damaged game fence. He was a nimble-footed little boy and back in school he was known as such. His small feet, oblivious of the sharp stones and twigs, hardly touched the ground as they virtually flew across the distance.

Just as he had estimated a few minutes earlier, he spotted the warden just ahead of him. His heart leapt in excitement at the sight of him but not for long. As he drew closer, slowing down into a trot, he noticed something unusual about the man. He was not moving at all. The warden was facing away from him and appeared to be concentrating on something in front of him. He did not even turn to acknowledge the arrival of the boy. The boy slowed down his pace into a walk, still panting from the run. At that particular moment, he saw it. He paused for a second or two and then walked on, treading carefully.

The snake had obviously spotted him and, judging from its reaction, it was not amused by the sudden intrusion. The hiss emanating from its mouth could have stampeded many a brave man, but it did not faze the boy. As a herd boy he had been called upon to defend his animals from snakes and rabid jackals. It was a job he always executed with pride and courage. However, what was before him now made him realize that he needed everything he could summon from his experiences to deal with the situation. In all his adventures, this was the first time he would have to kill a fully grown black mamba. He knew that the reptile was extremely territorial and any thought of it simply going away was wishful thinking. The situation was made even more complicated by the presence of the warden within striking distance of the snake. The reptile could strike the man at any time. From what he knew of the largest, most venomous snake in the wild, he was sure it had already struck at least once.

The snake was now swaying very dangerously while keeping an eye on both human beings. The boy continued to tread very carefully while moving towards the warden and snake, his hands preparing his bow and an arrow for the job at hand. He stopped just over eight metres out. The swaying snake presented a difficult target. Worse still, he could not afford to miss. Otherwise the snake would raise Cain immediately. There would be no time for a second attempt. There was yet another problem. The position of the target was very awkward, to say the least. A good shot was going to miss the warden's head by less than a metre. The only factor in his favour was that there was no wind. A clean shot in high wind would have been impossible.

The boy raised his bow and arrow, ready for an opportunity to let loose. At that precise moment, the snake made what turned out to be a fatal mistake. For some reason, it stopped swaying for several seconds. It was as if the snake was trying to make up its mind about something. The boy took a deep breath and aimed with his left eye closed. He remained in that position for the best part of what could only amount to three seconds, not daring to release his arrow without assurance of a good shot. Then there was a twang and a whoosh as he let fly the arrow. The long steel-tipped and feather-tailed agent of death flew horizontally towards its target like a bullet. It missed the warden's head by less than a metre all right. The boy did not release his breath just yet.

The snake saw the arrow coming and tried to sway out of its path but it was too late. The arrow struck its mark, the mamba's small hood, with the precision of a butcher's knife, the steel tip fully emerging on the other side. The deadly reptile went down, twitching and vomiting. The boy exhaled, leapt with joy and started running towards the warden and snake. As he reached them, the snake tried to rise but failed. The boy picked up a thick stick from nearby and smashed the mamba's head. The two people stood there for almost a full minute, watching the snake go through its death throes. Eventually, it became very still.

The warden turned to the boy and smiled. That was when the boy realized that the man had been struck on the left arm. The boy retrieved his arrow, wiped it clean with dry leaves, replaced it in his quiver and went into action before the man could say anything.

"Will you sit on the rock, mister?" said the boy, with the authority of someone twice his age.

"I thought that someone would never ask. You wouldn't believe me if I said my feet were killing me." Although the situation could not have been any more serious, John still tried to be humorous while taking his position on the rock.

"After what I believe you have been through I would. Let me have your belt." The boy was already tugging at John's belt even before he got a response.

"You can even have my left arm. After today, I guess I won't need it," he said, grinning. He was fascinated by the way the boy was working. The boy tied the belt just above John's biceps, got hold of the arm and started sucking the bitten part. He drew some blood and poison and spat them out. He repeated this twice and concluded that further suction would only make matters worse. Most of the poison had already gone beyond retrieval. He was sure that the belt would not help much but he was just doing what he had to do. He stood back and stretched out his right arm to shake John's hand.

"Hello mister, my name's Joe, Joe Sinyori. I was in the neighbourhood and when I heard the fireworks I came to investigate." The smile he gave John would have charmed a bird off a tree.

John could not help it but laugh. Here was a boy with a bright future. He wished he had met him during happier times.

"I'm Warden John Sithole. My friends call me John. You can call me that."

"Thank you."

"I should do the thanking. I'm sorry about this situation. I must have given you quite a fright."

"There is nothing to be sorry about. I have seen worse. Let's not waste any more time. The sooner we get you some help the better." Joe was already walking away from the scene of the encounter.

"My jeep is a few kilometres away," John said, picking up and holstering his revolver before following the boy. "I guess I can make it. We can then get back to Chipinda."

"How far will that be?"

"Given the terrain, it won't be very near. Unfortunately, there's no cell phone network. I can radio for our operation's helicopter once we get to the jeep but by the time it will get out there it may be dark."

"That settles it. We will go to my home and proceed to the clinic, which is not far from my home. There is also a phone in the clinic, a landline."

"Is the clinic likely to have anti-venom? I know we don't have mamba anti-venom in our camp. We have been waiting for new stocks for days."

"I don't know, we will see." The boy knew that John was already getting beyond the stage where any medicine would help him. By the time they would get to the clinic or beyond, it would be too late. After all, the Ndau Tribe did not call the black mamba "*Rasha Mutombo*" for nothing. Literally translated, it meant that once you were bitten by this snake, people might as well throw away any medicine they might think of administering. In other words, it was a waste of time, medicine and effort to try to administer any.

"Where did you learn the secrets of the wild?" John asked. "You seem to know a lot for someone of your age."

"I learned at home and in the pastures and woodlands. My father has been teaching me quite a few things about survival in the wild. I have also learned a few tricks on my own as a herd boy."

"Sounds like you have a big herd."

"Not anymore." The sad note in Joe's voice was unmistakable. "The drought has seen to that. By the way, tell me if I'm going too fast and I will slow down."

"The pace is OK."

"Like I was saying, the herd is almost gone. I look after the remaining animals more out of sense of duty than anything else. Today I will have to leave them behind. They won't go anywhere. There is nowhere to go. Even if there was, they wouldn't have the energy."

"What about cattle rustlers?" John asked.

"We don't have that problem here," Joe replied.

"By the way, how old are you?"

"Twelve."

"Do you go to school?"

"Yes, I'm in grade six."

"Well, the holidays will soon be over, and you will rest from herding cattle. What do you want to be when you grow up?"

"A doctor."

"That will be nice. From what I have seen today, it looks like you have already started on your practicals," John said, smiling.

Joe seemed to like this, for he also smiled.

As they crossed the game fence, John started to slow down. The amount of sweat he was losing had increased significantly. He was sure that his body temperature was now way above normal. However, he did not complain. He was not about to alarm his newly found friend just yet.

Joe sensed rather than saw the change in pace and responded accordingly.

"This nurse you mentioned," said John, "Does she live close to the clinic? By the time we will get there it will obviously be closed, and she would have gone home." He sounded a bit worried.

"Actually, it's already closed, but her house is in the same fence as the clinic. We will get there sooner than you think. Once we get home, we will get a donkey cart. Our donkeys are not yet as far gone as the cattle."

"Donkeys are hardy animals, like goats. They are usually the last animals to go in a drought."

"Do you want to rest?" Joe asked a few minutes later although he knew that, under the circumstances, it was not a very wise idea.

"No, let's keep moving," John responded. He could not quite make up his mind whether he was beginning to have double vision or it was just his imagination.

After what seemed to be a long time, according to John, they sighted Joe's home. At least Joe exclaimed that the hazy picture John was seeing ahead was his home. At that particular moment the warden felt a tightening in his chest and a severe headache that seemed to split his head into two. His vision became even more blurred and he started feeling dizzy. The burning sensation in his chest and throat became unbearable. Before he could say anything to Joe, he felt his limbs refuse to go forward. His knees felt like jelly and before he realized what was happening, he simply crumbled onto the ground. The last thing he remembered before he sank into a pool of darkness was why he was destined to die such a painful and cruel death and why all this should happen in front of an innocent twelve-year-old boy.

CHAPTER THREE

George of the Ambulance

George Nyarota was woken up by the music of his ringing cell phone. He grabbed it from the bed's headboard and placed it near his right ear while at the same time checking the bedside clock. It read 03:30. His wife of fifteen years stirred in her sleep but did not wake up. George was a light sleeper, a characteristic he had honed over the past seventeen years as an ambulance driver. Each time he went to bed, he knew that his sleep could be cut short any time. It was part and parcel of his life and he accepted that without any complaints. There was also another angle to this scenario.

George liked driving. As a matter of fact, if there was one thing he liked more than driving any other vehicle, it was driving an ambulance. It did not matter to him whether this was in the morning, afternoon or in the middle of the night: he always looked forward to it. There was something about the speed he could get his current ambulance to. He was fascinated by speed. In fact, George was fast with anything on wheels from a bicycle right up to a bus. The man could have been a race car driver if he had been offered the opportunity. Unfortunately, no one had been kind enough to offer. At forty-three years of age, he had since realized that this window had closed, and he had since decided to make the best out of the one he had. He had to be content with watching races on television and turning what he called his ambulance into a *de facto* race car. There was also something about the wailing of the siren and the dispersing of other vehicles on the road at his vehicle's approach that really gave him an adrenaline rush. Maybe he watched too many police-based movies.

"Hello, this is…," he said.

"Superintendent Mulenga speaking. I hope you have your shirt on," the voice from the other side said. He knew that voice even without mentioning of the name.

"Hello, boss. It can be arranged, boss," George said. He always joked with the hospital superintendent even though there their grades were miles apart. He especially liked the fact that Superintendent Mulenga was a likeable man who did not throw his weight around and could easily interact with his juniors, him included.

"Well, you better arrange for it right now. We have a Code Pari that has to be actioned pronto. See you shortly."

George knew what Code Pari meant a trip to Parirenyatwa Hospitals in Harare. That meant another seriously ill or injured patient. Since his house was close to the hospital, he did not need anyone to collect him. It only took five minutes to get to the hospital. By then the other hospital staff had already loaded the patient into the back of the ambulance. Two young nurses would accompany him to Harare.

"Evening, boss," George said on seeing Superintendent Mulenga.

"Evening, George. I hope I have not disturbed anything,"

George laughed.

"You sure did, boss. Unfortunately, I cannot go back to the dream I was having."

"Well, this is what you signed up for. Maybe one of these days that dream will come back to you."

"I hope so, boss. I guess we have another situation here."

"You can bet that shirt I talked about that we have. Give this your highest priority, George. It is a life and death scenario. Nurse Rachel will fill you in on the details. Nurse Frank will ride in the back with the patient. See you when you are back."

"OK boss, we're on our way."

Five minutes later, they were on the Chiredzi – Harare Highway. This road is very busy during the day, with buses, haulage trucks and other vehicles plying that route which goes through Zaka, Gutu, Chivhu and Beatrice before reaching the capital city. At night the story is a little different. You would be hard pressed to see any vehicle on this road for more reasons than one. There are very few people doing business during night hours. Most of the long-distance buses prefer to travel during the day for one reason or another. Most motorists give night driving a wide berth because of wild animals that roam the Chiredzi ranges and are inclined to cause accidents. So around three in the morning, the road is about as empty as a football pitch during the off-season. It is also as eerie at night.

George gripped the steering wheel of the ambulance as if his life depended on it. Perhaps it did. His eyes focused on the beam of light that continued to flee before them like a scared ghost. For some moments he forgot that he had passengers. The odometer hovered between one hundred and forty and one hundred and fifty within minutes. The siren was wailing all right. The only thing missing was the dispersing vehicles due to the time of the night. Everyone who was supposed to be on the road was probably asleep except an ambulance driver, two nurses and a man who looked more dead than alive.

"Do you have to go so fast?" Nurse Rachel who was still new to this kind of thing asked. She never really liked speed. "Speed kills," she had been taught. Of course, someone must have conveniently forgotten to teach her that speed sometimes saved lives.

"You call this speed?" George said without reducing. "You should have seen this machine when it was still new."

"There are wild animals out here, you know. Aren't you afraid that we might hit something?"

"It won't happen. I know this road as much as I know the back of my hand. There are indeed animals out here, but I have good reflexes. We will not hit anything." He was boasting.

"It would be a tragedy if we ended up in the back of the vehicles ourselves or elsewhere," she said, more to herself than to him.

"You're worrying for nothing. I have done this run a thousand times before. It should be a four-hour drive... not the standard five or six. We will be OK. Talking about tragedy, what do we have in the back?"

"Snake bite. They say he was bitten by a black mamba sometime before sunset."

"No kidding."

"No kidding."

"And you are sure that he is still alive."

"Surprisingly, yes, but barely so."

"He will die on us," George said but not out of fear. He had seen too much death in his lifetime to worry about another. To him, it would just be another statistic. "I know enough about black mambas that I know he can't live."

"He seems to be a fighter, though. He has lived for more than eight hours. They say that with black mamba you can't last that long."

"Indeed, you can't. Most actually die within two hours."

"The worst part of this job is that we have no black mamba anti-venom and so none was administered to him."

"My point exactly; he will surely die on us. Have you ever had someone die on you, not in a hospital setting but on the road like this?" He was deliberately trying to frighten her.

"Not really." She was not sure about where this conversation was going, but something told her that she was about to find out soon enough.

"Allow me to tell you a little story." He did not wait for her to respond. After all, it was not really a request. "One day during my second year on this job we were asked to do a Pari run. We had a man who had been poisoned while drinking a local brew in one of the villages. The trip was early in the morning, just like today, and it was my third trip to Harare. We started off well, but just before Chekenyere things started happening right there in the middle of nowhere. We did not have these little intercoms and I had one nurse who was riding in the back with the patient. Suddenly I heard banging sounds emanating from the back of the vehicle. He paused for maximum effect.

"You're scaring me."

"Be afraid; be very afraid, for stuff can happen out here. So far that is not the scary part. I stopped the vehicle and went to investigate. Apparently, the patient was dying, and he was not going quietly. He was staring at some unseen person or thing screaming that it should not take him. In the light of the ambulance cabin, the expression in his eyes was something straight out of a horror movie. It was the scariest thing I had ever seen. The nursed jumped out of the ambulance and started running down the road towards Chiredzi over sixty kilometres away. I was confused. I didn't know whether to chase her or to remain with the patient." Again, he paused for more effect.

"What did you do?" Rachel asked with a voice that sounded like a croak. She was petrified with fear, but she was curious. In any case she knew that this storyteller would not stop till the fat lady sang.

"I quickly realized that if this man was dying, the worst thing that could happen was to have some wild carnivore pay him a visit......and in case the back door was open...it would maul him. He could not be killed twice, but I would be damned if I was going to lose a nurse too. So I took off after her. Then I could really fly. You should have seen me in my heyday. I caught up with her in no time at all. I had to shake her a little bit to bring her back to her senses. Then I virtually dragged her back to the ambulance. By then the patient had died. The nurse would not sit in the back again and there was no need. After we had got back into the vehicle, I simply turned it around and headed back to Chiredzi. That is the end of my story. How do you like it?"

She just scowled at him before saying, "I hate it. I'm sure you told me this just to scare me."

"Did I succeed?" George had actually told a tale based on a true story but had added his own spice to it.

"I guess you did."

"Hahaha," he chuckled. "I have more where that came from. If you need another, I can always tell you. We still have the rest of the night ahead of us. Something tells me that you have had enough for one day, though. Let us change the subject then. What do we talk about?"

"Let us talk about anything else other than people dying on the road at odd hours and nurses running in the dark."

"Talking about nurses, let us talk about you."

"What about me?"

"Perhaps we should know each other better. It is too much of a long journey to be strangers. In my own weird way, I have already told you about myself. What I know about you is just that you are a nurse who is scared of dying people. I thought your kind was made of much thicker skin. Just how did you get into this profession?" He was teasing her again.

"I can hold my own, but circumstances vary. To answer your question, let me start by saying that I have always wanted to help people. Maybe it is also historical. My grandmother was a nurse. My mother is also a nurse.'

"Family business, ha?"

"You might call it that. It was not my first priority, though. I wanted to be an air hostess. I always felt that helping passengers while hung up at ten thousand metres above sea level was the ultimate sacrifice. Anyway, with a struggling national airline…..well, you know the rest. When the opportunity to do nursing came, I just continued with the family tradition."

"Wow, that is some story. So you are not that scared after all. Ten kilometres above sea level, you said?"

"Yeah, that is my adrenaline rush. I might be scared of one or two other things, but I am definitely not afraid of heights."

"Perhaps in my next life I should drive an aeroplane."

"Sorry, there are no aeroplanes up there."

"Do you really think there is a God?"

"Yes. I do not only think there is a God; I know there is a God." Rachel sounded very confident.

"How do you know?"

"Because the Bible says so and…….. look at everything on earth. Look at the Universe. Look at how organized it is; the sequence of things…the sun….the moon…..the winds…..the tide…..life itself and so forth. That is no coincidence. That is not from some Big Bang theory or monkeys changing to human beings stuff. It shows the hand of something bigger, someone bigger, the creator." She was on firm ground on this subject.

"But what about all the bad stuff…..like this guy getting bitten by a black mamba for example. Why does this God allow that to happen?"

"We may not really know, but God always has a purpose for what transpires in our lives, especially if we are close to him."

"And you think he is in control of everything."

"Yes."

"Well, he better be in control of this situation at the back because, like I said before, he is a dead man." George said that with the finality of someone saying that the case was closed.

CHAPTER FOUR

The Praying Mantis

Priscilla watched in horror as the unusually large scorpion approached Sam's hand. The creature was about as big as its target. She had never heard of a scorpion of this size, let alone seen one. If one was not right there in front of her, she would not have believed that anything like it existed. It was black all right, about as black as coal. The legs were long and strong, and the creature powered forward with the appendages with ease. The progress was somewhat slow, but this was more out of intent than anything else. It was as if the scorpion was afraid that its target would suddenly disappear. It need not have worried. The hand appeared to be there to stay. As the scorpion got nearer to its target, its stinger, which was hoisted in the air like a miniature crane out to carry a heavy load, started to quiver with excitement.

Sam was unaware of his predicament. He was completely absorbed in his fascination in the goldfish in the little pond in the centre of Harare Gardens. Priscilla was a few metres behind where he was kneeling. She was not sure why she was there instead of being beside her brother who appeared to be unaware of her presence. Priscilla had a spooky feeling about the whole atmosphere. There was her young brother sitting by the pond looking lonely and lost in his own fascination. There was no one else in the park, a very unusual situation on any afternoon. The place was as quiet as a graveyard at night, as if the noise of the city had been muffled by some giant silencer. There was something else. Apart from the two siblings, the scorpion and fish, there was no other living creature in the park. The trees, lawn, flowers and lilies were all dead and dry. All this presented Priscilla with the most eerie atmosphere she had ever encountered. No one could blame her. The atmosphere could have stampeded Count Dracula, the vampire.

Priscilla remained where she was, behind her brother, watching the scary scene unfold right before her eyes. The scorpion was getting dangerously close. She tried to move forward, but her limbs refused to respond. Her knees felt like jelly. It was all she could do to remain on her feet. She thought of shouting to warn her brother, but the voice stuck in her throat. Priscilla knew that a sting from the creature would most likely kill her brother. Sam was her only brother and she felt alarm at the thought of losing him. Her eyes started to moisten. The scorpion was now a few inches away from its target. Priscilla just stood there, her cheeks now wet with tears streaming from her eyes. The scorpion got within striking range and made its move. Priscilla realized that there was no way she could stop the course of events. She knew that, as surely as it was meant to, the sharp stinger would find its mark and her brother's fate would be sealed.

As accurately as Priscilla had imagined it, the stinger struck. Sam's reaction was as horrifying as the event preceding it. Priscilla expected her brother to jump up screaming in pain. He did neither. He simply fell over backwards and lay still. For a second or two, his sister continued to be a helpless onlooker, not having the energy to galvanize her limbs into motion. Then the energy came to her in a flash and she went berserk.

She ran across the short distance, her eyes on the black scorpion. The look in her eyes told the story of what she meant to do to the creature. However, this was not meant to be. By the time she reached where Sam was, the scorpion was already dead. She was completely astonished at the sudden turn of events. She wondered what had killed it. Priscilla sat down, raising her brother's head so that it would rest in his lap. She was not sure of what to do next as she stared at her brother's face. Eyes half-closed, he tried to smile, the first sign of his acknowledgement of her presence. He did not quite make it. He only succeeded in coming up with an ugly grimace. Then he started to convulse so violently that she could hardly hold him. She lost her nerve, somehow found her voice and started to scream, "Nooooooooo!"

Priscilla woke up screaming. For a few seconds she continued to scream, not realizing that she had been dreaming. Then, quite suddenly, she stopped and became fully awake. Her body was drenched in sweat and the flimsy nightdress she had on was soaked in places. Her face looked agonized, as if she was still in the nightmare. Her bedside clock told her that it was nine o'clock. Dimly she wondered whether she had not disturbed the neighbourhood.

Before she sat down to think about the nightmare, she went into the first thing she did every morning, praying. In fact, if there was one thing Priscilla did more than anything else in her personal life, it was praying. Her prayer sessions dated back to her first days in nursing college at Parirenyatwa Group of Hospitals when her current best friend, Helen, introduced her to the Christian faith. After this she never looked back. She made prayer her major asset. By the time she reached her final year, she had earned herself a nickname. They called her “The Praying Mantis”. The name stuck to her like a tick even after she graduated.

On this particular Thursday morning she finished her long prayer, slipped out of her nightdress, put on a morning gown and found her way to the bathroom. She emerged from the bathroom half an hour later and went to sit in front of her dressing table. She sat there for a while not doing anything except thinking about the nightmare. She could not figure out what it meant. Maybe it was just one of those dreams, she thought. But she felt that she would only feel at ease once she talked with her brother. She decided that she would phone him once she was through with her makeup.

She phoned Sam a quarter of an hour later. Her brother turned out to be, as he put it, as fit as the proverbial fiddle.

***

A few minutes after one that afternoon, Priscilla found herself walking up Mazowe Street towards Parireny-atwa Hospitals. Lost in her thoughts, she was humming the tune “Nearer My God to Thee” under her breath. She sounded like a bee out to collect pollen from a hibiscus flower. She was going on duty at two and so would be quite early since the hospital complex was nearby.

Now, as she walked with the grace of a cat towards the main entrance of the hospital, her brown shoes clicked on the sidewalk, making a few heads turn in the process. Those whose heads turned liked what they saw. You could not blame them. Priscilla was a beautiful young woman of twenty-four years of age. The beauty of her face was enhanced by the smile she usually carried. It was a smile that could charm a bird off a tree. There were times when she would have that smile even when there was really nothing to smile about. It would still hang on her lips like an unwanted child at a doorstep. If her smile did not get to you, then her eyes would. They had a kind look that suited her profession. Priscilla’s structure would also make most women green with envy. She was slim, without being too thin, the kind of body that suited modeling but without the skeletal appearance of the western models. She was a tall young woman, being close to six feet in height. Her nurse’s uniform could not hide her athletic build. As a matter of fact, during her high school days she was indeed an athlete.

At one time she had sent shock waves within the sporting fraternity when she smashed the national record in the one hundred metres dash. Had her parents not stopped her from pursuing what they called “unrewarding ventures” and ordered her to stick to her books, by now she would have at least made it to the Olympics. Her dark and lovely hair, which the nurse’s cap could also hardly hide, looked good on her.

Priscilla did not seem to notice the attention. Her mind set on other things, she continued to walk on with the sort of dutiful atmosphere which would make any patient feel better even before treatment was effected. At the intersection of Mazowe Street and Josiah Tongogara Avenue she walked right into the street, not realizing that the traffic light had turned red and other pedestrians had stopped. Priscilla was not the type of person to make that type of mistake. She had lived in the city long enough to know that such behaviour only contributed to an early grave. But then, when something is meant to happen, it will happen. Care or lack of it does not even come into it.

There was absolute pandemonium as horns started to blare, tyres screeched and brakes squealed in the ensuing fiasco. Drivers could not help it but shout obscene words at the nurse who stood right in the middle of the road looking bewildered by the sudden turn of events. Other pedestrians just watched in horror as car after car passed, missing her by inches. Those who muttered something agreed on one thing. The young woman had a death wish.

During the first few seconds Priscilla looked apparently shocked by what was happening. Then she quickly recovered, her profession's nerves of steel coming into action. She knew that her only hope was to remain right there in the middle of the road. Her expression changed from that of shock to one of detachment, as if nothing was happening around her, as if she was not even there.

As suddenly as it had started, the drama ended with the change in traffic light to green. Everyone heaved a sigh of relief. Priscilla and the rest of the pedestrians resumed their interrupted journeys. An elderly man caught up with her and started speaking with her. He had a slight limp in his left leg.

"That was a close shave," he said.

"As close as it can ever be," she responded. "I don't know what is wrong with me today. This came out of the blue."

"That is how accidents happen. You don't prepare for them. They come out of the blue. That's why people call them accidents."

"I guess so. I should still be more careful next time. I don't really have an excuse for this. Mind you, it could have been worse."

"Consider yourself lucky, young lady. Such an incident does not usually happen without tragic consequences," he said.

"It was just one of those things. I was at sea," she responded.

"It surely looked like you were. People in your line of work don't usually do that. It is the worst thing you can do in a busy street. It happened to me once, but I was not as lucky as you. Maybe I should say I am lucky to be alive."

"What happened?" asked Priscilla, feeling comfortable talking to the old man.

"I was also absent-minded. I walked into the same scenario as you did right in the middle of the city. Unfortunately, I made a second mistake. I panicked and ran. One of the passing cars hit me and I landed on the sidewalk. It is unbelievable, but that saved me actually, because landing on the sidewalk meant other cars could not hit me. Had I landed in the street I'm sure I wouldn't be talking to you today. I won't bother you with the details. You're a nurse, you can guess the rest. Suffice to say that three months later I emerged from hospital with this limp that has stuck to me like a birthmark."

"I'm sorry."

"Don't be. At my age you don't want people to feel sorry for you."

"OK, I won't feel sorry for you then. Don't feel sorry for me either, I've seen a lot worse."

"That is just fine with me. But don't do that again. If you've got something on your mind, find someone to talk to."

"I may do just that."

"One word of caution though, mind who you offload your problems to. For one thing, you don't want to appear in the tabloids," the old man said, laughing.

Also laughing, Priscilla looked at him more closely. She guessed he would never see sixty again although his hair appeared to be putting up quite a fight. His dental formula was still intact. She was not quite sure whether all the teeth were original or he had dentures, though.

"Thank you, it has been nice talking to you," Priscilla said, as they went through the hospital gate. "I feel a lot better already," she added.

"It has been nice talking to you also, see you around," responded the old man, "I really need to get to the Physiotherapy Department by half past one. Otherwise they will start thinking I'm not coming." He turned left to head towards the physiotherapy wing.

Priscilla turned right towards the main building of the hospital complex, called Sekuru Kaguvi. She could not help it but reflect on what had happened a few minutes earlier. Why was she absent-minded? Then it hit her. She had been thinking about the dream. She was still baffled by what it meant. If only she knew of the previous day's events of some five hundred kilometres south-east of the capital city, she would not have been as baffled.

***

At exactly half-past one, Sister Priscilla Makuyana walked into the duty room of D Ward, a smile hanging on her lips, like someone who had just received good news. It was a marvel that she was still smiling despite the almost fatal incident she had run into less than a quarter of an hour earlier. But then, the young lady knew when to frown and when to smile. A hospital ward was hardly a suitable environment for the former. So by the time she walked into D Ward, Priscilla, also encouraged by the old man's words, was already in a good mood.

Three nursing sisters, Felistus Mangena, Dorothy Mlambo and Helen Khumbula, sat at their desks chatting and waiting to help the incoming visitors. There were quite a few visitors as the visiting hour was at its peak. They all looked cheerful and approachable, two very important things in the medical field. As Priscilla walked up to their desk, Felistus spoke before anyone else did.

"Guess who has come in. If it is not our wonder girl, I'll be damned."

"Gimme a break, I'm nobody's wonder girl, "responded Priscilla who knew that her colleague had a flair for exaggerating that could have easily earned her an excellent political career had she ventured into that field. Yet she liked her very much. In fact, everyone else did.

"Don't think so lowly of yourself, Florence Nightingale. Otherwise everyone else will follow suit,'' said Felistus, with a smile which showed that she was really enjoying the conversation.

"Really, Felistus, sometimes I should never listen to you. You seem to live in a dream- world where every nurse is Florence Nightingale," said Priscilla who knew that this conversation would go on for as long as Felistus was in charge of the situation.

"You couldn't have been nearer the truth," chipped in Dorothy, smiling. "Sometimes I don't listen to her myself. The other day she called me Mother Theresa, of all people. I don't know what I'd done to deserve that. As you all know, I do not want to go and work among the poor in India, I'm nowhere near eighty and I definitely don't wish to die a nun!" Dorothy said the last bit while standing up. She made a modeling posture with her head held high and a mischievous look in her eyes.

All four girls laughed for close to a minute. Dorothy was tall and thin, about the same height as Priscilla, with the body of a European model. Those who did not know her would be forgiven for thinking that she was always starving, which was far from reality. Indeed, she had wanted to become a model. Unfortunately, her face betrayed her, suffice to say that she would never win a beauty contest. However, like Festus, to some extent, she was also a comedian.

"Hello Priscie," said Helen after the laughter. "You are certainly early. No wonder Felistus is getting carried away. Come to think of it, I don't even think that's the reason. She always gets carried away."

"It is just under thirty minutes to go," said Priscilla. "If you girls think that's early, then you either joined the wrong profession or someone has been feeding you girls with wrong information about the civil service."

"The way we work in this ward you would never think we were in the civil service," Dorothy said.

"You might have a point, honey," Helen came back. "We are civil servants who are practically in private practice since we deal only with private doctors and patients. This ward was created as such. However, this is what nursing should be like. To use Felistus's example, but not her beliefs, of course, Nightingale was kept on her toes most of the time and she was certainly never late for work. She also worked late into the night. It is no wonder that today we still read and talk about her."

"Well, I'm not here to prove some point or break some record. I'm just here to do an honest day's job and I wouldn't care a hoot if my successors remembered my name or not," Felistus stated her case. Listening to her, those who did not know her would be inclined to think that she was lazy. That would be misjudging her, for she was quite a bundle of energy. This was amplified by her short and stocky stature, with a handsome face that completed a structure and features that were more masculine than feminine.

Priscilla drew a chair and sat down facing the other three nurses after putting her handbag in the Sister-in-Charge's office. Her three colleagues were scheduled to knock off at two. Priscilla and two other nurses, Mirriam Mabhunu and Sandra Ndlovu, would assume duty then. The latter group would knock off at eight, after which the night shift would be in place until seven the next morning. Just as Helen was Sister-in-Charge during her shift, Priscilla was also in charge during hers. The two best friends were very responsible. Their work was also made easier by the fact that their colleagues were, like them, also responsible. It was a case of two perfect shifts. However, there were rumours about the third shift.

"I guess you girls have had a good day. You look so cheerful," Priscilla changed the subject.

"You can say that again," said Helen rolling her eyes that most men found attractive. Helen was a few centimetres shorter than Priscilla but still presented the image of a tall lady when she was standing. She was also beautiful, of good character and very pleasant to work with.

"We always look that way, Priscie. Looks can be deceiving," Dorothy added. "We have just had our most hectic day in weeks. This is our first break since we came in. And, believe me, we needed it."

"Really?" said Priscilla. "What's been going on?"

"I don't want to repeat myself on this one," said Helen. "I will wait till the other girls arrive. They should be coming in any minute now. People say that curiosity killed the cat. I know that you are not really a cat, but I surely hope you won't die, honey. Suffice to say that we have a situation in Room 22."

CHAPTER FIVE

Valley of the Shadow of Death

The electrocardiogram bleeped softly but distinctively, indicating the continuous beating of the Room 22 patient's heart. Though the bleeps were low, the sound was so exaggerated in the otherwise quiet room that it sounded more threatening than reassuring. The monitor showed a zigzag green line moving across the screen, indeed confirming the patient's heart was still functioning. The solution from the drip system soundlessly found its way into the patient's bloodstream, trying to inject a new lease of life where such life was almost gone. The supplementary respiration system ensured the patient's breathing was adequate. The intercom close to the patient's bed looked ready for use, but it appeared as if this particular patient would never get a chance to use it. The bed itself was neatly made. There were several other items in the room which showed that the place had been turned into an intensive care unit.

Sister Priscilla Makuyana stood beside the bed, flipping through the papers attached to a clipboard, her mind absorbing what she was going through. This was the last stop of her first tour this afternoon. Her two colleagues had already come to the room and left. After getting a detailed description of the situation in Room 22 from Helen, Priscilla decided to focus more attention on the room and its patient than anywhere else, hence the decision to make it her last port of call. And now, half an hour after leaving her desk, she found herself having to deal with this particular patient.

Priscilla felt some degree of sadness creeping over her as she went through the notes and graphs. She knew that Helen never exaggerated. As Helen gave her what she knew of this patient she was sure that Helen could not have been more accurate in her description and of the situation in the room. But still, as she read, it appeared worse than she already knew. Now after reading she gathered all the facts of the patient's ordeal and memorized them. Eyes still focused on the papers, but her mind elsewhere, she relived the full story in her mind as she now knew it.

The patient, John Sithole, had been brought in from Chiredzi Hospital, some four hundred and thirty kilometres south-east of Harare, arriving just after eight that morning, suffering from severe shock and acute snake poisoning. He had been bitten by a black mamba the previous day. By midnight, he had been admitted in Chiredzi Hospital. Efforts to raise mamba anti-venom in the hospital's pharmaceutical department had proved fruitless. Contacts with nearby hospitals and clinics had also yielded nothing, whereon the decision to dispatch the patient to Harare had been made. An ambulance had then sped northwest to the capital during the early hours of that morning with a patient who looked more dead than alive.

On arrival at Parirenyatwa Hospital, a heavy dose of black mamba anti-venom had been administered to the patient, more out of formality than anything else. Both the doctor and Helen's team, who had just come on duty, knew it. By the standards of many venomous snakes, it was too late to administer anything. Yet this particular man had not been bitten by just another venomous snake. He had been given the kiss of death by the largest, most venomous snake in Africa and any application of medicine at this time was about the same as trying to revive a corpse. All the same, the medical team had done its job. By medical ethics, a person was considered dead only when certified so. Other than that, hope or no hope, everything which had to be done to save a life would be done. By the time the doctor left for a break and Helen and her team took theirs, there was nothing else they could do except wait for the dark moment when all mortal life ceases and the spirit goes back where it belongs and flesh waits to fill a hole in the ground some six feet deep.

The nurse's eyes shifted from the papers on the clip-board she was holding to look at the man's face. It was very dark. The dark complexion looked somewhat unnatu-ral. Then she got it. She remembered that black mamba poi-son tended to darken the skin. There appeared to be some-thing handsome about the face, though, a phenomenon which must have been more apparent during happier times. The transparent oxygen mask and the relevant accessories made the atmosphere look slightly better than it really was. The patient's eyes were partly open but they did not appear to be seeing anything. Priscilla knew that indeed this pa-tient was seeing nothing. It was just like the sightless gaze of a corpse whose eyes no one had bothered to close. His lips were parted but his teeth were clenched; the expression of a man in extreme pain. His breath was still there but very shallow. The atmosphere in the room would have stam-peded anyone who was not in the medical field. For Priscilla, this was just one of those things. She had seen dif-ficult and terminal cases before. Parirenyatwa was a refer-ral centre. That meant most of the difficult cases found their way to the hospital. Her training had made her to develop nerves of steel.

The electrocardiogram continued to bleep, the sound reminding her of a time bomb. It might as well be. Priscilla was a deeply spiritual and hopeful person, but she knew when to accept reality. There was no way the anti-venom would reverse the fate of this man. It was a miracle that he had lived for more than twenty hours. Now, the shadow of death was upon him. It was just a matter of time before the bleeping would stop and the dreaded flat sound which signified cessation of the patient's heart would set in. Then it would be curtains for the obviously young man.

Priscilla shifted her eyes away from the man's face and replaced the clipboard and papers in a holder at the bottom of the bed. She turned away and started walking out of Room 22. Then she stopped dead in her tracks as something at the back of her mind started to become clear. The image of her dream started flooding her thoughts. She turned to look back at the man in the bed. Maybe she was clutching at straws but maybe she wasn't. It surely looked as if this was the "brother" in her dream and the story she had heard had some parallel with the dream. Just as she appeared to be failing to revive her brother in the dream, there was also nothing she could do about this man either. All the same, "The Praying Mantis" would still go through the ritual of what she did best in a crisis.

***

Priscilla Makuyana was not the only person who was concerned about the patient in D Ward's Room 22. His doctor was equally concerned. It would be the understatement of the year to say Dr Joshua Murdoch had had a hectic day. He had virtually been inundated by the day's activities. Earlier that morning he had been roused up from sleep by the shrill ringing of his phone. He checked his watch. It was a few minutes after three.

"Hello," he answered after picking up the receiver, his voice full of sleep.

"Hi Josh, it's Max. I hope I'm not interrupting anything," said the caller, who knew that he was indeed interrupting something. You don't call someone around three in the morning and not expect to interrupt something. All the same, the caller liked pulling his colleague's leg any time he got a chance to.

"You can say that again. Son of a gun, do you know what time it is?" responded Dr Joshua Murdoch with a rue-ful smile.

"As a matter of fact, I do, but who said anything about time? Someone in our line of work should know better than to complain about it."

"Yeah, despite that, some of us are not owls, you know. We enjoy a good night's sleep." Dr Murdoch enjoyed his sleep all right, but he worked any time of the day, sleep or no sleep. There was no harm in complaining if the opportunity arose, so he felt, albeit not seriously so.

"Tough luck, Josh. After I tell you my predicament, I guess your sleeping hours will be over for one night. You know me and my late-night calls."

Dr Murdoch knew Dr Maxwell Mulenga all right. The two physicians were friends. Their friendship dated back to their university days. Dr Mulenga was a general practitioner based in Chiredzi. Besides working at the general hospital in the town, he also ran a small private clinic in the town. Dr Murdoch was a neurosurgeon who ran a private surgery at the Medical Centre in the capital city. Whenever the need arose, some of his patients were admitted in Parirenyatwa's D Ward. The two doctors had a neat arrangement. Whenever Dr Mulenga ran into a problem that required a neurosurgeon, he would refer the patient to his friend. The neurosurgeon in turn referred his patients and friends from Chiredzi to Dr Mulenga for treatment of general ailments. The two still managed to travel and socialize in between their busy schedules. There was one thing Dr Murdoch knew, though. His friend did not usually call at this time of the day or, more correctly, night, if it was not an emergency.

"Something tells me that I'm not gonna like this call," said Murdoch. He regretted losing his sleep all right, but he was happy to hear from Mulenga anytime.

"I don't like it either," responded Mulenga, "Look Josh, I've got a situation out here. A game warden was bitten by a black mamba some ten or so hours ago. He arrived here at midnight. I was already in bed by then. Unfortunately, we could not do anything about his condition. We have been out of mamba anti-venom for some time. You know the crisis the Ministry of Health has been experiencing lately. There is hardly any drug in general hospitals."

"He's still alive?" Dr Murdoch was very surprised, although he had known more unusual things to happen during his lifetime.

“Believe me or not, he is alive. He is unconscious, though. In fact, he is in a coma. But heck, I’ll be damned if I don’t try to get help. I have already tried to secure anti-venom from Hippo Valley, Triangle and Masvingo hospitals but without success. They also don’t have stocks.”

“You must be getting old. You have already wasted three hours on your part. I don’t have to mention the fact that time is critical in this situation. What do you want me to do?”

“I’m dispatching this patient to Parirenyatwa Hospitals, D Ward. I want you to handle the case.”

“I’m not sure I’m the best person for the job. By now he must be suffering from all sorts of things. Forgive me for saying this, but by the time he’ll get here what he’ll need is an undertaker. From what I know of the black mamba, he should have died hours ago.” Dr Murdoch was serious.

“Yes, but miracles do happen, Josh. If by any chance, however remote, he gets to Harare while he is still alive, I want you to work on him. You know what black mamba venom does to the nervous system.”

“I’ll try to do what I can,” agreed Dr Murdoch. “I don’t wish to rub it in,” he continued, “but it seems we really have a situation all right.”

“You see, Josh, do more than just trying. My head is on the block. Although the three hours we have already lost may not make a difference given that he had already lost seven by the time he got here, the wolves may still descend on me. There are quite a few people who hate my guts and have been waiting for me to slip up. They will grab at anything to have me out of this place. I’m not scared of them or anyone else for that matter, but I won’t give them the pleasure of seeing me leave this place due to their effort. I’ll leave when I want to. Right now, I’m staying.”

“As if it will set your mind at rest, I’ll tell you not to worry. But some people must be crazy. You think they can fix you for losing someone who has been bitten by a black mamba? That reptile has enough venom to down several men at one go.” Dr Murdoch sounded both concerned and a bit angry.

“Like you said, they are crazy. I wouldn’t put anything past them.”

"OK Max, do what you have to do on that side. I'll handle the rest. I will be waiting for him, bye for now," said Dr Murdoch.

"Bye," said the voice on the other end of the line and there was a click as the speaker hung up.

Dr Murdoch followed suit and went into action.

***

Dr Joshua Murdoch sat in the canteen brooding over his cup of coffee, casting a lonely figure in a virtually empty canteen. This was the first break he had had in three hours and it was set to last only a quarter of an hour. He had not had breakfast, but he was not hungry. It was getting close to lunchtime, but he did not feel like having lunch either. The coffee would have to do for now. There was something about coffee and Dr Murdoch. Both the nurses and junior doctors he worked with had a saying: "Dr Murdoch is married to his coffee." This was frighteningly close to the truth because you could take anything away from the esteemed doctor but if you took away his coffee you and he would have words.

"Hi Dr Murdoch," the junior doctor who had been assisting him interrupted his thoughts. "I see you are almost through with your coffee. I thought I should join you."

"Be my guest. I'll be done in a few minutes."

"I won't take long either. I have done what you said I should do, but there are a few more errands I'll do after this break."

"You are a good doctor, Tim."

He meant it, for Tim was one of the brightest junior doctors at Parirenyatwa.

"Thanks, Doc."

"Anything on your mind?" Dr Murdoch knew that Tim always took advantage of any opportunity to learn.

"Yes, Doc. This case puzzles me."

"Me too."

"You see, most of his vital organs have shut down, except the heart, of course, that is barely beating."

"That is the nature of the human body. Everything else will go first. As you know, in the absence of medical equipment, the ultimate pulse to check when we really come to it is the femoral artery inside the upper thigh. That will be the last to go. With medical equipment we always check the heart, of course."

"What is your prognosis?"

"Not good, I must say, and I'm aware you have also concluded that. How he survived up to now, including the journey from Chiredzi, baffles me."

"Doc, do you believe in God?"

"That is an interesting question but let me put it this way. I am a scientist and therefore I believe in science. You should too. However, once in a while I meet cases like this one which make me question what I believe. Last year before you joined us we had a guy who was brought in here from Bulawayo who was critically ill. I remember his name was Thabani or something. He died on the operating table. I mean, I personally confirmed his death. He was put in the mortuary. Some ten hours later the mortuary attendant heard screams. Apparently, the guy had risen from the dead. I'm sure you heard about the story. There was pandemonium as people tried to make sense of what had happened. Now how do you explain that? Like I said, sometimes I do question what I believe in or more correctly, what I do not believe in."

"Well, Doc, it looks like we need another Thabani miracle right now."

CHAPTER SIX

The Swing of Death

Some twelve hours later, Dr Murdoch was still very wide awake and alert. He had cancelled all appointments for the day at his private surgery due to his latest patient. Everything that needed to be done had been done. There did not appear to be any change in the patient's condition. It was now time for nature to take its course. Even as Dr Murdoch walked into Room 22 for the twentieth time that day, he knew that there was very little hope for the patient's survival. Probably by some unknown force or willpower to live, he had refused to die so far. He had held out long enough as it was. It would not be long now.

"Afternoon, Dr Murdoch," Priscilla greeted him upon his entry, pulling him out of his deep thoughts.

"Afternoon, Sister, any new developments?" It was just a formal question whose answer he already knew.

"There doesn't seem to be any. I gather you've just had a long day."

"You can say that again. If you are through, I will fill you in on any details Sister Khumbula might have left out."

"I'm through, we can use my office," she said, whereon they went to the Sister-in-Charge's Office. After settling down in comfortable chairs, the doctor started the discussion.

"Sister, have you ever dealt with a patient who was bitten by a snake before?"

"Once, but then the snake was not even poisonous. We treated the patient for physical injury and shock. I know that poisonous snakes are another kettle of fish," answered Priscilla.

"You bet they are. I have seen this before. Most snake poison will, among other things, damage the nervous system. That's where I usually come in, as you know. In many cases I can help. Unfortunately, this particular case is not one of those."

"I'm told he ran into a black mamba."

"Yes. Believe me when I say that it is the worst thing that can ever happen to anyone. I lost an uncle back in 1979. He was in the Rhodesia Front. One day he went out on patrol against Zanla guerrillas. He had a whole platoon with him. When he left camp, he did not know it then, but he was destined for the toughest fight of his stint in the army. It also turned out to be his last. You might think that he ran into guerrillas. Far from it, he encountered his worst nightmare. The story was that he ran into one angry black mamba which vented its anger on him and his colleagues. Know how much it cost to kill it? It took three men and a bullet. My uncle was the first to go. He died within two hours of being struck. The second man died an hour later while on his way to hospital. The third died on arrival at the hospital, some four hours after being struck."

"Sorry about that." Priscilla's sympathy was genuine.

"Don't be. I hate to say this, but they got what was coming to them. They were fighting an unjust war. Anyway, to get back to what I was talking about, the black mamba is the most vicious of all snakes in the wild. Unfortunately, it is also the most venomous, well, at least in Africa. As a matter of fact, the boomslang has more deadly venom per unit volume. The good news about this small snake is that it has a small volume of poison and it will only bite you if it has to. What makes the black mamba so dangerous is that it is extremely territorial. Most snakes will slither away to safety at the slightest opportunity. The Mozambique spitting cobra will try to frighten you away with its impressive threat display, a raised head, spread hood, hissing and spitting. But if you move away to look for a weapon you are likely to find it gone by the time you get back. Not with a black mamba. If it raises its head and sees you in its territory, even at a distance, you better see it and change position fast. Otherwise within seconds it may be right next to you and swinging at you. It is that aggressive. Many people call its strike, 'the swing of death'. This is because very few people have been caught by that swing and lived to tell the tale."

"Why do people call it a black mamba?" asked Priscilla. "I know it is either brown or grey."

"Because of its mouth," answered Dr Murdoch. "The name has nothing to do with the skin colour, unlike in the case of its less vicious but still poisonous counterpart, the green mamba. The mouth of the black mamba is black. The snake's full name is black-mouthed-mamba, black mamba for short."

"I see. What exactly does the poison do? What characteristic symptoms are exhibited by the victim? I know I have seen some of them today."

"Yeah, you have already seen some of it today. However, by the time this patient arrived here he had gone through a lot. If you are bitten, you feel the pain and shock of the fangs and poison entering your flesh and bloodstream. Then the poison starts working on anything in its path. It digests flesh, attacks the nervous system and breaks down blood cells. Before long you feel nauseous, headache and dizzy. Chances are you will start vomiting then. Systemic poisoning symptoms appear within an hour. Your muscles become paralyzed rendering them non-functional. The jaw and tongue are paralyzed as well, making speech slurred initially. Speech stops as paralysis becomes complete. Copious amounts of saliva ooze from the mouth. The eyelids will be drowsy and yet difficult to close. The pupils will just stare and register nothing with disappearance of sight. Breathing becomes laboured and extremely painful. A victim does not usually last ten hours at the most. Most victims will die in less than half of that time and it is not a very nice way of dying, if ever there was a nice way of dying."

"Well, this one has lasted almost a day," said Priscilla, who felt goosebumps on her skin with Dr Murdoch's chilling description.

"That is what is baffling me. I can only think of two possible reasons. Either he is very strong or deep in his subconscious is a willpower to live. The latter might just be sustaining life where actually life is more or less gone. But I'm sure he won't last long now. I don't see him getting out of the coma." He hated to say this, but he was a realist and professional talking to another.

"That sounds so final." She was not disputing the fact. She just found it very painful. "So all we have to do is to wait." It was not a question.

"I'm afraid so. Well, Sister, I've had a long day, as you mentioned earlier. I haven't taken anything since four this morning, at which time I had a cup of coffee. Let me go to the canteen and grab something solid."

"If what you have said is true, you need more than that, Doc."

"I guess you're right. I'll see,'' he said and went out.

***

On that same Thursday afternoon Michael Chiponda hurried up Robson Manyika Street on his way to Parirenyatwa Hospitals. His mind was full of unresolved issues which looked likely to remain that way until he saw his colleague – alive. He was also not sure whether the last visiting hour of the day had started, or worse, had come and gone. His wristwatch told him it was a quarter to five, but that did not really mean anything for as long as he did not know the visiting schedule.

The previous night Michael, together with his colleagues, had been roused from sleep to be told that John was on his way to Chiredzi Hospital. Michael and Constance were not really asleep. They could not. The chilling report which had been brought by one of the wardens from Chipinda wiped away any feeling of sleep or lethargy which was creeping up on them. Michael was a man who did not take ages to make up his mind. And, once it was made up, it took quite an extraordinary development for him to reverse his decision. He told his colleagues that he had made up his mind to go to Chiredzi. He packed a small bag, commandeered a vehicle from Chipinda and took off with a colleague, Paul Masoni. Although he was not quite decided on the need for the bag, something at the back of his mind told him that he was going to need it. Michael was also the kind of person who, when he was not a hundred percent sure, would take the safer option. He had never had regrets about this type of thinking in his adult life.

Michael and Paul arrived in Chiredzi some two hours after leaving the temporary camp. The news that greeted them was neither good nor bad. John was already on his way to Harare. Michael asked his colleague to leave him in Chiredzi and go back to the game reserve. Michael had already reached another quick decision. That same morning, he would take the earliest bus to Harare. He went down to Tshovani Township to Reverend Baloyi's house. He roused the old man and his wife from sleep and gave them the bad news after which all three went into a lengthy prayer before going to bed.

Michael woke up hardly two hours later to prepare for his trip to the capital city. He got the earliest bus all right. He expected to arrive in Harare by two in the afternoon. Unfortunately, this was not to be. The bus broke down just after Jerera Growth Point, some eighty kilometres from Chiredzi. By the time the mechanic arrived and fixed the problem, the bus was already two hours behind schedule. Hence Michael Chiponda found himself arriving at Mbare Bus Terminus, Harare's main bus terminus, just after four in the afternoon.

He soon found himself in the city centre and into the so called "Avenues". Now, as he crossed Fife Avenue, he knew that he still had Baines, Chinamano and Tongogara avenues to cross before he reached Parirenyatwa Hospitals. The streets were now very busy, with pedestrians and motorists starting to find their way home after a long day's work. The young man seemed oblivious of all this, his mind set on what he was likely to see once he arrived at Parirenyatwa.

Michael entered Parirenyatwa hospital premises using the pedestrian gate of on the western side of the hospital complex. He walked eastwards up a narrow tarmac road as if he meant to eventually branch off to the Dental Centre. He missed the Centre by turning left about fifty metres from the gate and started walking towards the largest building of the hospital complex, Sekuru Kaguvi. This building housed both public and private wards, an outpatients' department and part of the University of Zimbabwe's School of Medicine. As he walked on, he could see the maternity wing, Mbuya Nehanda, on his right.

In a few minutes he passed the Senior Staff Cafeteria and soon found himself at the main entrance of the hospital block. There were a lot of people entering the building, which meant that Michael was in time for the visiting hour. He walked past the massive reception area and proceeded to the elevators. He entered one, together with other people who literally jammed the elevator. He rode up to D Floor. In a few minutes he was talking to one of the ward's nurses. She ushered him into the Sister-in-Charge's Office. It was a typical hospital office, very neat and spacious, and smelling with drugs and antiseptic. The nurse behind the big desk in front of him looked up and smiled. It was the sort of smile that could charm you even if you were in a mood.

"May I help you?" she asked politely. "Oh, you can have a seat," she added, as if it was an afterthought.

Michael instantly liked her. Maybe it was the smile or maybe it was her attitude, he could not quite put his finger on it. All the same, she presented a good image of her profession. Where he came from, half the nurses frowned more often than they smiled.

"My name is Michael Chiponda. I'm from the Department of National Parks and Wildlife. I'm based in Gonarezhou Game Reserve. I understand you've got a colleague of mine under your care. He arrived this morning, snake bite." He felt as if he was not talking to a stranger. Priscilla had that effect on people.

"Yes," she said, and then added, "I'm Sister Priscilla Makuyana. I guess you've already been told the latter."

"Yes."

"Are you his relative or friend?"

"Friend, we work and socialize together. He's also the leader of our church home group," answered Michael.

"I see," said Priscilla, who knew a lot about home groups. "Does he have any relatives?"

"A few, but they are not that close. He is an only child and his parents died in a bus accident while he was still in high school."

"Then I guess there is no one else in Harare who will visit him."

"There are several colleagues from our Head Office here. Other than those there is no one else."

"I see. Do you intend to stay in the city then?"

"Yes, I'll be around for a while, depending on developments."

"That's very nice of you."

"Thanks, may I go and see him now?"

"Of course, he's in Room 22. It's the last door on your right as you go down the corridor. But before you go let me tell you about his condition. You might as well brace yourself for it." So Priscilla told him about John's condition.

An hour later, Michael emerged from D Ward, rode down the elevator to the ground floor and proceeded to the reception area. He pulled out his cell phone from his pocket and made two phone calls before he left for the high-density suburb of Highfields where his eldest brother lived. He phoned Pastor Baloyi first. Four minutes later he was talking to Constance who, together with the rest of team, was already back in Chipinda. The message he got from the two was the same. They had proclaimed a fast. The message he gave them was also the same. John was in a coma.

CHAPTER SEVEN

The God of Elisha

The church hall was packed to the rafters. The hall was meant to sit three hundred congregants but had gone well beyond that figure. Extension would have to be done soon. Anyway, who was counting and for what purpose? Suffice to say that anyone associated with this church had turned up for this so-called "Big Sunday". Maybe it was the excitement of the monthly event. Perhaps it was an unusual increase in faith and the sheer need to renew commitment to the Lord. Perhaps this was driven by the need to get together in the face of a tragedy that had befallen one of the flock out there in Gonarezhou National Park. John was a brother who was liked by everybody. Whether it was during bad times or good times, you could count on him to be there for any member of the flock. Now that the shoe was on the other foot, everyone kept saying, "Lord, not him." Yes, perhaps that was it. Maybe there was also news of developments up north. Everyone was just waiting to hear something, be it positive or negative.

On his part, Pastor Baloyi was worried. The first thing he was worried about was the state of the young man over four hundred kilometres away. Pastor Baloyi was a man of faith. It took quite a lot to worry him. Right now, he was worried all right. Yes, in all his thirty years of service to the Lord he had witnessed the hand of God work miracles in his life and the lives of many other people, saved or not. He had seen seemingly impossible situations turned around. He knew that this God he served, this Jesus, would never be defeated. He thought about the last time he had had a big challenge such as this one.

Some two years back, one of the congregants had brought a dying child to his house. The mother was weeping but she said something remarkable. She said that she believed that if, through Pastor Baloyi, Jesus wanted, He could heal her child. By any standards, this was an unusual request. He knew that if he encouraged the woman and her wish was not granted, there would be a price to pay. Normally a person in the child's condition needed to be in hospital. The government was very strict on that. If the child died in his house and the information leaked to the authorities, he would land in hot water. A few weeks back a pastor in another church had attempted to resurrect a dead person and the miracle did not happen, the media had had a field day and the authorities raised Cain. Within a week he had been banned from being pastor and subsequently arrested for fraud. At the same time Pastor Baloyi also knew that the denial of someone's faith was not healthy for the flock. He was therefore pretty clear about the consequences of his actions either way. Nonetheless, without much hesitation Pastor Baloyi had called on the God of Elisha. The miracle happened: the child recovered fully, and everyone lived happily ever after.

There was a second thing that worried the Man of God. He had procrastinated to go to Harare. If only he had gone there, perhaps his worries would have lessened. For the next few days he was still tied up with other church business and could not quickly head north. He really wanted to lay hands on John. He was sure that calling the name of the Lord did not necessarily mean physically touching the patient, but something at the back of his mind kept saying that he should indeed go out there and do so. He also knew how this would look if he did not visit. The congregation would talk. Yes, many were saved but that did not stop gossip. It was as if, somehow, the same mouths had remained dry during baptism by immersion.

Yet there was a third and more immediate issue on his mind. The singing and dancing congregation meant everything was building up to the Word and he was due to deliver. For the past few days he had scoured the scriptures for something to present but nothing seemed to stick. It was only early that morning when he had felt drawn to the theme of the God of Elisha, not for the first time in his life. Something in his spirit said that this was the kind of message for such a time as this. Still he was not sure, though. He remembered the "fear not", the "do not be afraid" messages he used to preach. Well, he said to himself, he needed to continue practising what he preached. In any case, if this message was from God, it would be God speaking and any embarrassment, if it happened, would not be Pastor Baloyi's.

Now the praise and worship was ending. In a few moments he would be on the pulpit. He braced himself for the occasion. He looked at his wife and smiled. Susan smiled back at him, giving him reassurance that all would be well. After thirty years of marriage, she still had it. You would not believe that she had given birth to five children. They also had three grandchildren. Susan was his best prayer mate and confidante. He had not talked about this issue, but she knew as a mature wife and prayer warrior would. After all these years of marriage, she knew him more than anyone else on earth. She had sensed his apprehension but she was sure God would take him through as usual.

Now he was on the pulpit. After the usual formalities he went into his message.

"I do not usually want to preach about current affairs but today you will forgive me. Today we have a situation that has affected one of our own. You have all heard about it by now and I am persuaded that you have been praying for our brother John. My wife and I have been praying too. When one of us suffers, we all suffer, Amen!"

"Amen!" The congregation answered in unison.

"We are the body of Christ. If any part of the body has an injury or is not doing well in one way or the other, the other parts cannot have peace. We cannot have peace when John is out there in the valley of the shadow if death.

Our theme for this year 'Nothing is impossible with God' seems to be prophetic. It comes from Luke 1 verse 37. Things may be impossible accord-

ing to the human mind but with Him, all things are possible."

"Amen!"

"Amen!"

"I am reminded of the God of Elisha from the second book of Kings Chapter 4 verses 8 -37. Can someone read it for us?"

A youth stood up and read while the whole congregation listened. When he finished, the Man of God continued.

"That is the God I know. He is a God who resurrected the son of the Shunamite woman from the dead. The Bible says that weeping endures for a night and joy comes in the morning. Weeping turned to joy when the boy was restored to life. Yes, we might agonize over our friend's ill health, but joy will come to us too. Our God can do it. He is a God who gives us hope when all hope is lost. As people we reach our dead end. With Him, there is no dead end. He is also the God of Abraham, Isaac and Jacob. Some of you might ask, why the God of Elisha? Let me explain. Jesus said that John the Baptist was the greatest prophet who ever lived, be-

cause he prepared the way. Note that he came in the spirit of Elijah. His successor Elisha received a double portion of Elijah's anointing. That is why he performed the second highest number of recorded miracles after Jesus. If you forget anything else about Elisha, remember this one thing: he was so anointed that long after he had died, his bones resurrected a dead young man when his body touched his bones. Due to the raging war people had put him in Elisha's tomb, there being no time to dig a grave. The young man was restored to life just by the touch of those dry bones. I am not talking about the dry bones in Ezekiel Chapter 37. Those were another set of dry bones. I am talking about the dry bones of a dead man of God. That is what this God can do.

"He is the same God who opened a way for the Israelites to cross the Red Sea. That was a situation of being between a rock and a hard place; the Egyptian army on one side and the Red Sea on the other.

"He is Jehovah Rapha, the Lord who heals us. No situation is beyond him.

Trust in him. Let him intervene in our situation.

Whatever happens to a Christian, happens for a purpose.

"He is the same God who healed Naaman of leprosy using the same prophet Elisha.

He defeated Goliath through the hand of a seventeen-year-old boy, David."

His voice was building up to crescendo.

"He is the same God who gave us Jesus Christ!
By his blood we were saved!
By his stripes we were healed, says the word of God!
He resurrected Lazarus from the dead!
Mary and Martha, the sisters of Lazarus, had given up!
They said that it had been four days and so it was too late.
Let me assure you today!

It is never late for Jesus and He is never late!

He is never late! Jesus is always in time or on time!

Have faith, have faith, have faith!"

"Amen!" the congregation was in the flow.

"He is the same Lord that raised the cripple at the gate of temple through Peter and John!

He had been crippled for 38 years but that did not stop his healing!

It had been 38 years, but when he was healed, he jumped with joy and ran into the temple!

He is the same Lord who raised Dorcas from the dead after the widows testified of her goodness!

Let us raise testimonies for our brother today!

We all know his works!

Yes, we all know that when the time comes, we go back to our maker!

Yet today we say, 'Not like this, Lord!'

You are with us today, Lord!

He is with us today!

He is the same yesterday, today and forever!

Behold his hand is not shortened that he cannot heal, nor are his ears deaf to the pleas of his children, says His Word!

"I proclaim and declare healing in the name of Jesus!
I proclaim and declare complete recovery in the name of Jesus!
Satan, you're defeated!
Satan, you're defeated!"

People did not even wait for Pastor Baloyi to make an altar call.

***

More than four hundred kilometres away in the north of Chiredzi, a related incident was playing out in Pastor Irene's

office. The pastor was one of the few female pastors of her church, but she had no problem with that. As a matter of fact, with the ministry, she felt like a fish in water. She knew who had called her into the ministry. It was Him she was accountable to, and her flock and Overseer, of course. Everyone simply knew her as Pastor Irene. She was a thirty- six-year-old widow with three children. Ever since her husband had died some five years before she had never looked back. That road accident might have robbed her of her husband and best friend, but it had not robbed her spirit.

Priscilla had walked into Pastor Irene's office after the service, having signalled to her earlier that she wanted to talk to the woman of the cloth. Priscilla liked her and vice versa. Many a time Pastor Irene had given Priscilla strength when she felt down in her spirit. The pastor especially liked her because she was very active in church affairs when she was away from her busy hospital schedule.

Priscilla never liked to take her work home but once in a while she would make an exception to her rule.

"Shalom, Pastor Irene," Priscilla said upon entering the office.

"Shalom, Sister Priscilla," the Woman of God answered.

"Nice sermon, Pastor," Priscilla said after settling in a comfortable armchair in the office.

"We thank God for that, Sister Priscilla. It is always a challenge to keep up the standard especially at the end of a week-long revival. But God is faithful."

"He is indeed."

"I'm sure you did not come in to talk about the sermon. What is on your mind?" Pastor Irene did not believe in beating about the bush.

"Well, I am worried about the case I talked to you about earlier. I know we prayed about it and I am still praying, but it just has me worried."

"You know what they say, 'Worry is like a rocking chair. It keeps you busy but is does not take you anywhere.'"

"I know, but I can't help it, Pastor."

"It is understandable, but what is your main worry? He has lived so far."

“I am worried that he may not pull through. His body is under siege, though we have managed to stabilize things. Things just look so grim.”

Pastor Irene gave her habitual encouraging smile and said, “It is when things are so grim that the hand of God shows itself. Let me tell you a little Biblical story. You probably know about it but for what it is worth, I will retell it anyway. Once upon a time during the era of the Prophet Elisha the Syrians besieged Samaria, which was then capital of Israel. The siege was so bad that there was virtually no food in the city, the Syrians having cut all supplies, with no one coming in or going out. The idea was to starve the population of the city until they surrendered. When I say ‘bad’, I mean ‘bad’. It got to a stage that in even heads of donkeys and dung of doves were sold at exorbitant prices. I mean, the children of God ended up eating things declared unclean by the Lord then. It got worse. They even had at least one publicized case of cannibalism. Two women agreed to eat their own children. They ate one, but on the day that they were supposed to eat the other the mother hid the child. These women even had the audacity of bringing the matter to King Joram. The King tore his clothes in anger and instead of dealing with the problems he started finger pointing. He blamed Prophet Elisha for the siege and vowed to have him beheaded. You would think that was the end of both Israel and Elisha. Far from it.

"In all this doom and gloom, Elisha did not panic. He calmly predicted that the next day God would intervene and there would be plenty of food in Samaria. You know how God intervened? He used four men with leprosy to defeat the Syrian Army. Where am I going with this story? I just want to show you that it is when we have nowhere else to run to that God intervenes. He does not have to when we are capable. He specializes in those things that seem impossible to us. That God of Elisha who lifted the siege of Samaria can surely do the same for us today."

"Thanks for your encouragement. I have read that story before but never saw it in that light."

"I'm glad to hear that. That God of Elisha is also our God and He will grant us the desires of our hearts."

They went on to talk about a few other things church folk normally talk about. The most important thing was that when Priscilla left the presence of the Woman of God, she was less worried.

CHAPTER EIGHT

The Man Who Came Back from the Cold

Six weeks later, Sister Priscilla Makuyana still found herself walking into D Ward's Room 22 on the same errand at eleven in the morning. The worry was back again. It had been a long time since she had that conversation with Pastor Irene. Her face was unusually grim, and her thoughts were back to trying to solve an otherwise impossible problem. She had been on duty since seven. In two days' time she would change to the afternoon and evening duty. A week later she would be on night duty. Then she would have a rest for a week while on her nights off. Quite often, she looked forward to the vacation, which was understandable given some of the hectic days she experienced in the line of duty. Now she liked the night shift but did not look forward to the subsequent vacation. She felt as if she wanted to remain on duty forever. It was as if going away was a bad omen, as if it would bring something tragic to the patient in Room 22. It was as if she held the lifeline of this particular patient. For days she had been battling with the notion that she was obsessed with her work and especially in relationship to the coma patient. Was it just work? She was not sure. Or was she?

Now, as she walked into the room, she was greeted by the sight which had become all too familiar – the prostrate figure of a man who looked more dead than alive. At least he was not dead yet as everyone expected, she thought. His condition was critical but stable. No one knew whether he would snap out of it, which was unlikely, or give up the ghost. Dr Murdoch continued to visit him, but not as frequently as during the first two weeks. He had asked ward staff to contact him if there was any new development in his absence. From the way he said it, everyone knew that the only development he expected was definitely not positive.

John's friend, Michael Chiponda, had gone back to the south-east Lowveld three weeks earlier. He too had realized that his stay in the city and frequent visits to the hospital were serving no purpose. He too seemed to have lost hope. All the same, he would continue to intercede for his friend, if it was the last thing he would do, he vowed to himself. Priscilla had talked to him a lot during his visits. She found the young man likeable. There was an atmosphere of sadness to the tales he told. Not that they were all sad. Some of them were even humorous. However, they were overshadowed by the present. Each time she looked at Michael and at John for that matter, she wished she had met them during happier times.

Prior to John's arrival, Priscilla had directly dealt with a coma patient only once in her medical life. That was two years after she graduated. The patient had been brought into D Ward following complications caused by a variety of opportunistic diseases that took advantage of her HIV positive status. By then she had full blown AIDS. The young lady had lived in denial for a long time and things eventually caught up with her. She was in really bad shape and it was a wonder that she was still alive even when she was brought in. It was sad to see such a young lady in that position. The saddest part of it was that, one week after lapsing into a coma, she suddenly seemed to give up the fight for her life. On that fateful Saturday morning, as the night shift was about to go off duty, she passed away.

Priscilla relived the experience in her mind as she stood close to John, subconsciously examining him and jotting down the usual indecipherable jargon only medical staff could read. She wished John would not meet the same fate. She knew, of course, that wishes were not horses. If they were, beggars would ride.

Priscilla did not know it then, but the day's events in D Ward were destined to take a new twist.

***

Priscilla and Helen sat in the Senior Staff Cafeteria, sipping orange juice dessert and discussing the usual things single ladies normally talk about. They had a lunch meeting and hence Helen had come early. She was scheduled to start work at two, at which time Priscilla would knock off and go home. The two met often for lunch, though their sometimes hectic schedules made things difficult. Helen had actually requested that they meet on that particular day because she wanted to have a heart to heart with Priscilla. For days she had had a funny feeling that something was in the air and there was one only person who could tell her exactly what it was. Helen was the sort of person who, if she felt that she was onto something, would never let up until she made a breakthrough. Right now, she knew she was onto something big and the moment of truth was just around the corner.

"How is the sleeping beauty?" Helen changed the conversation from what they were discussing, looking at her watch in the process. The time was twenty-five minutes to one.

Priscilla automatically knew whom she was referring to although her friend did not mention him by name.

"Still sleeping." There was a sad note in the tone of Priscilla's voice.

"Like a well-fed python, you mean?" Helen tried to bring back some humour into the atmosphere.

"I wish he was, well, sort of. I mean, if he was a python he would snap out of his sleep once the grub was digested."

"He has copious amounts of black mamba venom to deal with. I think he needs time. You know something? I'm beginning to think that he might live."

"You are beginning to sound very optimistic. I wish I was in your shoes."

"Don't flatter yourself, honey. You know that my shoes are too big for your small feet. You wear size six, don't you?" said the smiling Helen.

Priscilla could not help it but laugh. Here she was, looking as if the world was coming to an end, and yet her very close friend across the table was beaming from ear to ear.

"You know what I mean," Priscilla said after the laughter.

"I was beginning to think that it would take more than this to put a smile on your face. It wasn't so difficult after all. Anyway, look at it this way. This young man has survived this long. That in itself is a miracle. Doesn't that tell you something?"

"Maybe, but remember that girl from a few years back."

Helen also knew whom she was referring to.

"Look, you are not being professional. You can't make that type of comparison and you know it. After all, that was different. That was HIV/AIDS-related infections but here we are talking about snake bite. She did not live for six weeks, although she could have even lived for the rest of her life if she had made the right decisions in her life. He has lived for six weeks against all odds. In fact, he's the one who should have died within a week but, surprise, surprise, he didn't." Please don't wave this 'history repeats itself' stuff in my face. It doesn't cut any ice with me. It is overrated." Helen exhibited humorous defiance.

"Suit yourself."

"I definitely will. If you're as watchful as you should be, you'll see that this guy is a fighter. He has come a long way."

"That doesn't seem to be good enough."

"Hey, what's wrong with you? You seem to have taken this case very personally. You know we can't get very personal with patients. Is there something I'm missing? It can't be just the dream." Priscilla had told Helen about the dream.

"Why should there be? I take all my cases seriously."

"That's not what I said. I don't know, but hearing you speak, one would be tempted to think that you have a soft spot for that guy," Helen said smiling.

Priscilla knew that Helen was fishing. She also knew that it would take a bomb going off at close range to wipe the smile off Helen's face. Even then, she could not be sure as she had seen that smile in very bizarre circumstances before.

"Why would I have a soft spot for an obviously dying man?" asked Priscilla.

"Don't you think that I haven't been asking myself the same question? But I have seen you do weirder things than that. So I wouldn't put anything past you."

"I'll let that one pass."

Helen would not be shaken off so easily. It was her nature. Once she made up her mind to stick to something, she stuck to it like a tick. Many thought that if she had developed a flair for exaggeration, she would have made a good tabloid journalist.

"Ah ah! Not so fast. You are not getting away from this one so easily. You don't seem to realize it, but I probably know more about you than you do yourself."

"Don't get carried away, I am not trying to get away with anything. There is nothing to be fussy about."

Helen simply broke into laughter.

"That's exactly my point. You should listen to yourself whenever you talk about John, then you will know who's really fussing. This case has really got to you. The funny thing is that despite that occasional sad expression of yours, I like you better that way, girl."

"What way?"

"I'm talking about being emotional. At least the iron lady has feelings after all."

“Helen, you are really letting your imagination run away with you. No one is being emotional.”

“Fine, but why is it that I don’t believe you?”

“Maybe you are just being paranoid, as usual.” Priscilla was also smiling, feeling some advantage.

“Believe what you want to believe, honey, I don’t care. Something has definitely got to your heart. If I am wrong, Pythagoras was definitely wrong about his theorem.” Confidence oozed from Helen’s voice.

“What am I going to do with you?” Priscilla sounded as if she was about to give up.

“Simple, put me in front of a firing squad and you will hear no more from me.”

“I’m not even sure about that. Something tells me that you are likely to pop out of your grave to come back to hound me.”

“Very unlikely, but it wouldn’t be such a bad idea, though. I’m not sure that I will have any opportunity to hound anyone else in the after-life, but that’s beside the point.”

“What’s the point?” asked Priscilla, as if she did not know.

"I have already spelt it out, but I don't mind repeating myself. I have all the time in the world. It's you who has to rush back to work."

"I can believe that."

"You better. If you don't tell me what's going on, I will breathe down your neck till kingdom come."

"I'm sure you will. For as long as you don't breathe fire I don't mind. All the same, just to get you off my back……………………."

Helen sat forward in anticipation while her friend took her time to say her piece.

"Yes, go on."

"And, off the record…………….."

"Don't stall honey, keep talking."

"I kind of like that guy."

Helen's smile broadened. She remained quiet for several moments before pressing on.

"What do you mean by 'like'?" You like me, you like your uniform and you even like this orange juice, big deal! Put some more substance into this."

"I mean, really like." Priscilla was still confused about her feelings and hence she was hesitant to spell it out.

"You are getting close, but it's still not news yet."

“Remember this is off the record.”

“Yeah, you don’t have to rub it in. You know me better than that. Let me ask you this question. Are you becoming emotionally involved with John?”

“I’m not sure, I might be.” In fact, Priscilla was becoming more and more certain as she spoke about it.

“Holy smokes! No wonder you’re so dotty about him. Girl, you are really referring to comatose John?”

“Let me put it this way; between you and me and the orange juice, yes.”

All Helen could say, without losing her smile was, “I’ll be damned, I never saw that one coming!”

It was one of the few times Priscilla had heard Helen swear.

***

John felt being dragged by the undertow closer and closer to the whirlpool whose raging waters seemed to be in an uncompromising mood. His struggles were becoming feebler as he felt his energy completely overpowered by the swiftly moving water. How he had come to land in this predicament, he could not understand. He did not remember walking into the dam. He did not remember seeing any dam with a whirlpool right at its centre anywhere in his twenty-seven years. Somehow, he had noticed that this was a dam that did not appear to have any source of its water. The water happened to be there and was being sucked at the centre of the dam by some unseen force but without any sign of the dam losing water.

Now he was dangerously close to the whirlpool. The water was getting to his neck and he felt himself sinking and the water rising further. He looked around again but still found no one who could help him. The water was at his chin, his hands raised in a last gesture of a fight for survival that looked destined in one direction. He closed his mouth to prevent water entering as it rose to his lips. It continued to his nostrils. Now he was almost in the whirlpool. In a last-minute gesture before he started taking water in his lungs he craned his neck yet again so that he would have a last look at the sky. Something bright caught his attention. The thing looked like a shadow, but it gave the whole area extra illumination. The object descended rapidly and quickly and gripped his hand in a vice-like grip. It was then that he realized it was a hand. Before he realized what was happening, John felt himself being pulled effortlessly out of the water so that only his feet remained touching water. The hand released him, but he remained standing on top of the water. He looked to the east and saw what he had not seen earlier. An extra beam of light was apparent from where he was. It was shining straight from the sky and onto the bank of the dam where a large congregation was beckoning to him to come to where they were. They appeared to be very far away, but somehow he recognized quite a few faces in the crowd. At the head of the crowd was a beautiful young nurse who seemed to be more enthusiastic than her colleagues. He was sure she was a nurse. For some reason she must have failed to change her uniform and wear something more appropriate for the occasion, he thought. John found this very amusing and smiled.

A few seconds later he was heading towards the congregation, walking on water, the smile still hanging on his lips. Suddenly, he felt some irritation in his nostrils. He was sure it was nothing to do with dust because there was none around him. It was probably the light, but he was still puzzled. He knew that bright light tended to stimulate nostrils of young babies and make them sneeze. He had never heard about such a phenomenon in adults. The stimulation built up very rapidly and, before he realized it, he had sneezed three times.

***

Suddenly John was wide awake and realized that he had been dreaming. The world of a few seconds earlier had vanished like morning mist. He wasn't sure about what the dream was all about. All he knew was that he had a slight headache. After shaking his head a little, he concluded that it was nothing to shout about. His sight was slightly blurred but he could see that he was in what could only be a hospital room. He could not quite smell anything as he was breathing through some sort of funnel. Then he realized that he must be under supplementary respiration. He could hear the distinct bleeping of something. It must be the electrocardiogram, he concluded. Still he could not figure out where exactly he was and why.

John tried to rise but found the effort difficult. He decided to continue lying there for a little while longer. In a few minutes his vision became clear. However, he did not like the foul taste in his mouth. It was as if he had slept for a very long time or had gone for some time without food.

He felt something on his left arm and checked it out. He was under drip. Alarm bells started ringing in his mind. What was this all about? Had he been in an accident? How long had he been lying in this bed? Maybe it was an hour, maybe a day, maybe………… Something disturbed his thoughts. Footsteps were approaching his room and in a few seconds the door of his room silently swung open and a nurse walked in.

John gaped at the woman who had just walked in. She was beautiful all right and there was an air of charm around her. Yet that was not what made him gape at her. He had no doubt about the realization that had just occurred. He could not help gaping at her because she was the nurse he had just seen in his dream.

The nurse seemed to have been surprised to see that her patient was conscious, for she stopped just inside the room for a moment, her right hand flying to her mouth. But that was all there was to it, a moment. Priscilla quickly recovered her composure and completed the rest of her journey to John's bed and took a good look at him. Satisfied that the patient was indeed out of danger, she quickly removed the supplementary respiration system so that the patient could speak freely. Her movements were gentle and steady.

"I see that the sleeping man is awake. You gave us a bit of a fright," she said jokingly, as soon as she had finished.

"Although I'm not quite sure what you are talking about, I'm sorry." The corner of his mouth creased into a smile. His voice was a bit groggy but relatively fine, given the circumstances.

"I guess you don't, but you'll know in due time. All the same, welcome to our world."

"I've been in your world all this time." He found this conversation amusing.

"Tell me about it. If I didn't know you, I'd be tempted to believe you. I know better," she said humorously. She looked genuinely happy and she also looked very relieved. She was feeling as if someone had removed an impossible burden from her shoulders.

"I'm embarrassed. I hate it when beautiful ladies like you see me in this condition." John was not quite sure, but he thought he saw her blush.

Priscilla could not quite make up her mind whether he meant it or he was just teasing her. So she decided to play it safe.

“Don’t worry, Mr Sithole, our kind has seen a lot worse,” she said. “It comes with the job,” she added.

“So you really know me,” said John, more for something to say than anything else. It was not a question.

“I should. In fact, I have to. Otherwise I would be fired for incompetence. You are one of my patients, Mr Sithole.”

“I see. You can call me John. At least I remember my name. Beyond that I don’t seem to remember anything else. What is your name, Sister?”

“Sister Makuyana,” Priscilla answered, deciding to remain formal.

“That’s your title and surname, I guess. May I know your first name?”

“Even for a patient who has just made a comeback to real life you surely ask many questions.” She did not sound angry, only amused.

“If what you say is true, I should. If one has been away, he surely wants to catch up on things.”

“My name is Priscilla,” she said, throwing caution to the wind.

“Nice name.”

“Thanks.”

“Do me a favour, will you?”

“What can I do for you?”

“Can you tell me how long I have been in this neck of woods?”

“Don’t be shocked when I tell you.”

“Go ahead, make my day.”

“You’ve been with us for six weeks.”

John had braced himself for the answer, but it still gave him a bit of a jolt.

“What?” He could not hide his surprise.

“Yeah, you have had one long sleeping session, but thank God you’re back. You are really the man who came back from the cold.”

“I don’t seem to remember anything.”

“Don’t worry; it will come back to you.”

“Can you tell me what happened?”

“It’s a long story. Since you are now OK, I will alert my colleagues that you are back. Then I will call Dr Murdoch. I will then come back and fill you in on the details and see whether we can bring that memory of yours back as well.”

"Who's Dr Murdoch?"

"Like I said, you surely have many questions. That's another long story. Suffice to say that he's your doctor. Give me a few minutes and I will be back with all the answers to your questions."

Priscilla walked out of Room 22 and went to talk to her colleagues who received the news with excitement and went into action immediately. A few minutes later, Priscilla was speaking to Dr Murdoch who promised to be there within half an hour. Then she went back to John and began to talk.

CHAPTER NINE

Love is in the Air

The sky was rapidly becoming very dark, with the appearance of heavy nimbocumulus clouds signifying a pending storm. The heat had also built up rapidly during mid-morning and hence the resultant clouds. A lot of people were surprised at this development. For almost a year it had been very hot but these clouds seemed to have gone on strike. People had never seen anything like it in a long time. Now, the clouds were back and the type of storm that was brewing had all the hallmarks of Noah's era. People hurried for cover, realizing that it would not be very healthy to be caught out in the imminent storm. They had waited for this one for a long time, but they were not risking their lives for it. Some were rushing home, cutting short their shopping. Others were hurrying back to work, cutting short their lunch. Those who had not yet gone for lunch realized that they would rather fast than venture out into this impending storm.

Streaks of lighting crisscrossed the sky and thunder crashed, reverberating around the city as mother nature started her war games. The phenomena sent shock waves even in the less faint-hearted. Within a short time, the heavens opened up and it started to rain. In fact, "rain" did not best describe the scenario. It was pouring. The raindrops, which were large enough to knock a man out, pounded the earth with tremendous force. The few people who had had the nerve to venture out and try to enjoy the rain after the worst drought in living memory quickly changed their minds and hurried back to safety as rain continued to pour out of the sky as if from a gigantic drum that would never go dry. Within a short time, the streets were in flood and there was absolute pandemonium in the ensuing traffic jams also compounded by the near-zero visibility.

For one particular motorist, the situation could not have been worse. Michael Chiponda had driven at breakneck speed towards the capital city as soon as his office received a call that John was due to be discharged from hospital at midday. He, together with Constance and three other colleagues, had been to see John a week earlier. That was a week after he came out of his coma. They were relieved to see him well on his way to full recovery. In fact, he might have been released then had his doctor not insisted that he should stay another week for observation. Michael did not know it then, but John had used that week to get more acquainted with Priscilla. At least they had got to friendship level. Priscilla was a bit apprehensive about John's intention of taking the relationship to a new level. He was still her patient and the professional in her kept whispering to her to wait till the right time. She felt that mixing duty and pleasure would be a recipe for disaster.

Four hours after leaving Chiredzi, Michael found himself on the outskirts of the city. By half past twelve, he was right in the heart of the city, hence he found himself in the worst traffic jam in his driving life. The whole Julius Nyerere Way was in total chaos by the time he crawled to its intersection with Samora Machel Avenue. Then he got no further. A minibus had careened into another car, starting a chain reaction of events that eventually resulted in a complete standstill of traffic around the intersection following a pile-up. Although Michael's vehicle did not hit any and vice versa, he found himself hemmed right in the middle of vehicles with blaring horns and roaring engines. Despite all the fiasco, no one seemed to have been injured. The motorists appeared to have decided to sit the storm out or at least wait for the police to solve the headache. They were probably not even very hopeful about that either, for it would take a miracle to clear up the street in this weather. It was also advisable for the police to sit out this rain and act when at least the worst was over. That meant everyone would be late for his/her schedule. At least Michael knew that he would be very late for his. He hated to keep John waiting, but there was nothing he could do.

If Michael had known what John was thinking at the time, he wouldn't have worried. Things could not have been better. For him, Michael's late arrival was a blessing in disguise. He wished Michael would take longer. John was in perfectly good company and he did not want that to end.

***

At Parirenyatwa Hospitals, it was lunchtime visiting period and many people were already in the wards. They were not in a hurry to get out, even those who were here more out of a sense of duty than anything else. The storm outside was taking no prisoners and there was nothing they could do about it.

The hospital can be a very lonely place for a patient. You sit in your room or ward urging the clock to move faster to the next visiting hour. It can be a very frustrating experience, especially when that hour comes and no-one turns up. Of course, once in a while the medical staff will come in to say hello, check a few things or administer medicine. But that is not a source of comfort for, you see, the nurse might come in with a nauseating drug or a syringe in her hand. Now, that can be frightening if you are one of those people who can't swallow a pill or has a fear of needles piercing into your flesh. Yet, all this is for a good cause.

There was one man in the main hospital reception lobby who did not have to worry about all this. Just after midday, he had ceased to be a patient. That made him a very happy man indeed, but that was not his only source of happiness.

Two nurses had accompanied him to the lobby. Still there was more. One of them was in uniform and the other was on her nights off and so was in casual attire. It was the latter who was the source of most of his happiness. She had promised to see him off on his discharge from hospital and she was doing just that.

Helen sat with them for about a quarter of an hour before she said goodbye and went back to her work. Duty called, of course, but it was also a very convenient move. She could have stayed longer had she chosen to. Helen read situations very well. She knew when she was company. She also knew when she was causing a crowd.

"You are very close," John commented after Helen had left.

"Yes, we are. We've been close since nursing college. She also introduced me to Christianity," said Priscilla, feeling proud of her friend.

"She is very good, you know. You all have been very good to me." He was sincere.

"It's our job. We enjoy executing it," said Priscilla.

"It's more than that. Believe me when I give that compliment. It's not everyone in your profession who works like you ladies. I am not just talking about the work rate but also the hospitality."

"I don't wish to sound my own horn but I believe most staff members in our ward joined this profession because they liked it. That can make a difference. Some join a profession just because it is the only one available at the time of application. Probably half of those will eventually like the profession. The other half is another story. They might give our profession a bad name."

"You are right. I have seen both sides of the coin in my working life."

"So have I. Anyway, what are you going to do with yourself once you get back to Chipinda?" Priscilla asked. "I hope you are not going hunting for snakes once again out there," she added mischievously.

"I'm going straight back to work. Actually, the snake hunting idea is not such a bad thing if it means I have to come back here to be under your care."

"Don't count on it. Next time you might sleep forever. But seriously, I thought you were going on leave."

"I have been on leave during the past eight weeks. If I extend that, I'll become lazy." He seemed to be joking.

"That was sick leave, it's different. You need real rest."

"I'll see, but the idea does not appeal to me. It has started raining and so there is new work to be done."

"I'm beginning to think you are a workaholic."

"That makes it two of us. You don't know how many times I've thought about that."

Priscilla laughed softly. She was enjoying the exchange.

"I don't know about that. It's only a week and a half since your memory came back." She was just joking.

"You must also be right on that one." He was also not serious. "But I wish to take full advantage of that. If someone accuses me of saying something out of turn, I can always say that I don't remember."

"You are funny, you know that?" she said, laughing.

"So are you. But you are more than that. You are warm, kind, beautiful and charming." He meant it.

"Thanks, but I hope that's not one of the statements you will deny later." She was teasing him again.

"Well, I won't, scout's honour. I like you very much and I wouldn't do anything to hurt you." He was now very serious.

"That's what Delilah said to Samson before the haircut," she responded humorously, trying to steer the conversation from where it was obviously heading. It was not that she did not want it to head that way, eventually. But she did not want to rush into anything she could not handle just yet. Jokes were safer ground. Serious emotional discussions were more difficult to deal with.

John could not help it but laugh at what she had said. He went on for almost a minute before eventually coughing to a stop. Some tears of laughter had welled up in his eyes.

"You're quite something, you know that? Please spare my lungs. They are too fragile for this."

"Earlier on you were claiming to be fit enough for work and so you might as well face the music. All the same, you need not worry about your lungs. When we declare someone fit, we know what we are talking about."

"OK, but let's be serious for a minute." He gave her a chance to respond.

"I'm as serious as I could ever be," she said, but her smile suggested otherwise.

John realized that he would not get anywhere quickly if he did not drop the bombshell. Michael was late, probably due to the storm. Sooner or later he would turn up. John meant to have covered some good ground by then.

"Will you marry me?" He said this so quickly and so casually that if Priscilla had not been listening carefully, she might have missed it.

She heard him all right. If someone had given her a punch under the heart she would not have been as shocked. This one had come right out of the blue and she did not even know what to say. Of course, she had realized that he was interested in her. Maybe she expected a softer approach or maybe she did not even know what to expect. She felt like someone who had been waiting for something to happen and yet when it did, she was totally unprepared for it. She could not look him in the eye. She could not trust her knees and so she was glad that she was sitting down.

"But…………….," she stammered. "You know very little about me. You've known me for only two weeks."

"You've known me for eight, so I guess you can make a good decision. Besides, I know you well enough to want to marry you. I am a good judge of character. As a matter of fact, I feel like I have known you all my life."

"I hope that someone has not been gossiping about me."

"That's beside the point." John had casually talked to Priscilla's colleagues, of course. They had been a particularly good source of information, but he was not telling Priscilla just yet. "The point is, no matter what you think I know about you, I love you and I wish to marry you. I know, I might have got the sequence in reverse in the first place, but I can always use my usual excuse."

"You have really thrown me into the deep end. You seem to have thought about this. Will you give me time to think as well? You certainly have dropped a big one." The funny thing was that she had already made up her mind. She was just going through the hard-to-get ritual ladies enjoy.

"Much as I would like to leave with a better answer, this is a democracy, but promise to call as soon as possible. If you don't, I will call you soon. I have your home, cell phone and work numbers. Here is my business card," he said, dipping his right hand into his shirt pocket to retrieve a business card.

"How did you get my other numbers? I can understand the work one. My home phone is not even in the directory yet."

"I have my sources. Suffice to say that I keep an ear to the ground. You call me."

"I will."

"That's settled. Now we can talk about you," John said, changing the subject.

"But you said that you already knew a lot about me,'" she protested.

"I do, but I have known you for two weeks and you have known me for eight. It is time to even the score."

"I'm not falling for that one just yet. First let's talk about you."

"What is there to talk about? I was bitten by a black mamba, went into a coma, snapped out of it six weeks later and fell in love."

"You think it is as simple as that? Have you ever thought about how you survived? You were not supposed to live, you know."

"I have given it a lot of thought. I can only say that my miraculous recovery was due to the hand of God," he said with a serious note in his tone.

"I kind of agree with that."

"That is a good start, at least we have agreed on something." He was all humour again.

The conversation wore on and on. They seemed like two friends who had been together for many years.

When Michael arrived to find them still in the lobby at three that afternoon, it was still raining fit to drown a duck.

CHAPTER TEN

The Final Twists

Gonarezhou Game National Park, which includes Chipinda Pools, is one of Zimbabwe's tourist destinations that do not usually get the accolades they deserve. For some reason, Gonarezhou especially gets overshadowed by Hwange National Park. It is probably due to its distance from Victoria Falls, the top tourist destination in the country. Hwange National Park is much closer to the world-famous falls. It is a pity that Gonarezhou gets only a fraction of the tourists that visit its main counterpart, for it is a beautiful place to visit. Tucked away in the south-east of the country and covering over five thousand square kilometres, Gonarezhou ("The place of the elephant") is by any standards a large national park. The fact that Gonarezhou is not as heavily commercialized as Hwange makes it the perfect place for one who is seeking the ultimate wilderness experience. Most of the campsites are what they are, just campsites. You can bring the camping gear yourself or you can take advantage of the park's tented facilities, including at Chipinda pools. The pools are the Runde River. There are eight other campsites across this park. Chipinda Pools Camp happens to be the main camp of Gonarezhou. There are also some tents for the few staff of the national park. A much bigger tent is available for events that require accommodating up to a hundred people (seated). It is not every day that such events happen. This day happened to be one of those rare occasions.

On this particular day Michael sat on his veranda, contemplating his next move. The event planned for later that day was fast approaching but it was still at least two and a half hours away. He was excited about this event. He was even more excited by the fact that his friend John was back among the living. John was a friend who was closer than a brother and for that he was grateful of his good health. It had been a close call, though. Michael was not unfamiliar with close calls. They had been part and parcel of his childhood. Apparently, they had also followed him into adulthood.

Michael had grown up with a father who was a prophet. He had witnessed people healed in their house. They came with all sorts of ailments; physical, emotional and spiritual. They were all delivered from those ailments. Even people who had been discharged from hospital as terminal cases had received their healing once his father prayed for them. It brought a smile on his face that many years later, the same God who had healed many people he knew long ago was still working wonders. Yes, times had changed. The characters had also changed. However, the game remained the same. Apparently, the God he prayed to also remained the same.

Talking about "game", there appeared to be a new game he needed to play. His heart skipped a beat when he saw Helen come out of the house nearby to go and pick some flowers from the garden. The house belonged to Constance who was hosting two guests from Harare.

For some weeks now, Michael had not stopped thinking about Helen. Yes, they communicated frequently as new friends, but Michael felt something deeper. He also felt that, on the surface, Helen also presented herself as a friend, but if Michael scratched deeper, he might hit the jackpot. Unfortunately, there was little time for that. The schedule was hectic. They had arrived the night before. That morning they had been busy with whatever ladies are always busy with. For the rest of the day it was going to be difficult to isolate Helen. The ladies also needed to be on their way back to Harare the next morning. So talking to her the next day was out of the question. Somehow, he had to find a way to isolate Helen today or he would have to postpone. The latter was not an option, he thought.

His mind shifted back to the afternoon event as soon he saw Helen come out of Constance's tented accommodation. She had picked something from the veranda. He had waved to her and she had waved back before going indoors. Everything that had to be prepared had been prepared, but Michael had a feeling that something was missing from the equation. At first he could not a finger on it. It was as if he had an almost complete puzzle that needed just one missing piece. It was that piece which baffled him. After more mental gymnastics he got it. It was as clear as day now and he knew exactly what he needed to do. Michael needed to take immediate action. There was not much time; it would be a close call. If things worked well, he would be considered a genius but if he failed, he would be regarded as stupid and irresponsible. As always, once his mind was made up, even wild horses would not keep him from his target. Perhaps he could kill two birds with one stone, he thought, or perhaps even three. He just needed to convince someone first without giving the upcoming surprise away.

Michael braced himself for the job at hand. The talker in him gathered momentum. He knew for sure that he had two very good qualities in this regard. He could easily talk his way out of a jam. He could also talk his way into anyone's heart. Apparently, it was the latter that he needed shortly.

***

A quarter of an hour later, Michael found himself driving in the bush with Helen at his side. The lady was still a little mystified by the trip. Michael had given justification but despite agreeing to go with him, she was not quite convinced about his explanation. Helen being Helen, she started to dig.

"Where did you say you were taking me?"

"For a game drive," Michael replied, "I figured that with only a short time remaining for you in this neck of the woods, this is about the only time I can do this. I want to give you city girls a treat," he continued, smiling knowingly, his eyes on the winding narrow dirt road ahead.

“Girls, as in Helen and Priscilla? Well, I do not know whether it is my eyes or what, but are we not missing one girl?”

“I guess we are, but who is complaining? Look at it this way; you will have all the stories to tell your friend.”

“Yeah, a little selfish, but I can live with it. It would very unwise for Priscie to be late anyway…...in case we will be late.”

“My point exactly, but don’t worry about being late. We will be there in no time. Trust me.”

“Trust me,” Helen repeated his words, more to herself that to Michael. “The number of times I have heard that phrase. How can I trust someone who has just kidnapped me in broad daylight and is taking me to God knows where?” She was teasing him.

“What would be the ransom if I indeed kidnapped you?” Michael was also enjoying himself.

“How do I know? I’m the victim here. A million US dollars perhaps?”

“No, you are worth more than that.”

“Two million.”

“More.”

“Five million....and that is my last suggestion.”

"Helen, you are worth more than all the money in the world," Michael said, realizing that she had, in fact, presented him with an opening. "At least this is how I feel about you."

Helen did not respond immediately. After a few moments she did indeed respond but picking her words carefully, stayed on the humour course.

"And how much would that be?"

"You are priceless. Look here, Helen, I fell in love with you the first time I saw you. I love you now and I will always love you."

"Aha," she said, wanting him to say more.

"My dear Helen, I have just poured out my heart to you and all you say is 'Aha'?" He was actually amused by the response.

"Why do you love me?"

"You are the most beautiful person in the world...."

"And if you find someone more beautiful than me, you will move on?" she interjected, knowing full well that he wanted to say more. She was really enjoying this conversation.

"There is more. You are the most charming person I have ever met. I feel that the two of us are halves of one whole. We complete each other. You are the first person I think about when I wake up in the morning. You are the last person I think about at night."

"You forgot to say that you think about me in the afternoon." She was still being playful.

They briefly looked at each other and laughed.

"For a moment I thought you were not taking this seriously," Michael said after the laughter. He was still in a joyful mood.

"You said some deep words," she said.

"That is how deep my love is for you."

"The feeling is mutual," she said.

"Thanks for that," he said, exhaling forcefully.

"I knew you were getting me out here under false pretences."

"Not quite. With me what you see is what you get. I must add that what I say is also what you get. Though it will feel more like a fly-past, you will still get your game viewing and more. I can actually see the first herd of elephants in the distance."

Helen stared ahead until she saw Africa's giants referred to. It was the first time she has seen these majestic animals besides on television. They were a large herd, perhaps up to fifty animals. They were crossing the road ahead and going to some unknown destination elephants always go to. Now she will really have something else to tell Priscie. She was really going to be green with envy. Well, two things had played out so far. Perhaps there would be a third as per Michael's "more".

***

The lone skinny herd boy was back on his familiar anthill looking after his animals. The animals, two cows and two donkeys, were grazing the new green grass that had sprung up following the rains that had fallen over the past few weeks. To say that it had rained was a gross understatement. It had poured. Hardly a day went by without a downpour. Even today, a big storm was brewing but at least it looked as if it would come in the evening. And so he had ample time to herd his animals and be in a safe environment by the time the day's rains would come. Rain had brought back life from the brink. Even though his family and community had lost so much in the drought, this was now water under the bridge. The sound of people ploughing and planting filled the air. The only reason why his two donkeys were not on duty was that his family had finished ploughing and planting. It had not been easy with lands so wet, but they had stuck to it and completed. It was no wonder his facial expression was different this time. You could see the hope on his face. He had every reason to be this way. The skies had smiled at last.

Joe now herded the animals with renewed enthusiasm. He admired the way the animals' condition was improving with the abundant upcoming green grass. He wished more animals had survived the drought. Joe still carried his bow and quiver full of arrows plus the whip. He also carried something else these days. It was the bag containing John's camera. Since that fateful day he had kept custody of this electronic device and bag and never left it whenever he ventured out of his homestead. His parents had once asked him to leave it at home and wait for someone to claim it, but he politely refused, saying that he had better chances of meeting a game warden when he was out in the pastures. He did not want to use the camera. Neither had he even tried to. He just counted on meeting someone who could take it on behalf of John. When that would be, he did not know.

Joe kept wondering why no one had brought back any news or had come to claim the camera. Since that fateful day he had not heard anything. Almost three months had gone by since his encounter with John and the black mamba. He was convinced that John was dead. There was no way he could have survived a black mamba's bite. He felt sad at the thought. He had been a nice man and it was sad to lose such a nice guy like that. Maybe he should ask his father to go to Chipinda and find out. Maybe........... something stopped him from his wandering thoughts.

It was the sound of a vehicle. It seemed to be coming towards his home. He did not think twice. He simply climbed down the anthill and ran towards his home. By the time he arrived, the vehicle, a green National Parks Land Rover, had already stopped near this family's main house. He slowed down to a walk as he saw two unfamiliar people, a man and a woman, talking to his father and mother. His heart skipped a beat. He had looked forward to the visit for a long time. Finally, he would hand over the camera, but something scared him. He was sure the two had news about John. It was now time to close the chapter on John. It was time to hear the bad news.

***

That afternoon John's living room in Gonarezhou Game Reserve Chipinda Camp, was full to overflowing. It was four weeks after he had left hospital. All his friends, colleagues, fellow worshippers from Chiredzi and some relatives had turned up for the occasion which few people wanted to miss. Many had come to see a man brought back to life by what they could only describe as a miracle. They had come to celebrate his recovery with him. Pastor Baloyi was on hand to chair the occasion. Now, he was making the introductions. He had waited a little longer to get the party going so as to make sure that everyone who was supposed to be present was indeed there. When he realized that the two people who were missing would arrive much later than would be convenient, he pressed on with the day's programme.

John was beginning to get worried about the two missing people. He was flanked by Constance and another lady who was a complete stranger to most of the people present. He nudged Constance.

"Where's Mike?"

"I don't know." She knew. "Since he went out with Helen, he hasn't come back yet."

John turned to Priscilla.

"Is there something going on between those two?" he asked.

"What two?" Priscilla asked.

"Mike and Helen," he said.

"Search me." Priscilla suspected that something was either going on or was going to happen sooner or later. Since they had arrived a day earlier, Michael had been all over Helen. Helen did not seem to have a problem with the attention. In fact, Priscilla thought she was encouraging him. When Michael asked Helen to accompany him for a drive three hours earlier, she willingly obliged. Priscilla thought this was more than her friend's interest to see wildlife.

Further conversation was interrupted by the pastor who was calling John to the make-shift stage. He obliged, feeling uncomfortable that he was going to introduce Helen in absentia. He cleared his throat before addressing the audience.

"Ladies and gentlemen, boys and girls, welcome to the party. I know I have been asked to introduce special guests and so I will try to stick to that for the meantime. I will have more to say later. By any standards, mine is a fairy tale. For God did not only bring me back to life. He has also given me a life partner. Let me introduce to you, my fiancée Priscilla Makuyana……….." He did not even finish.

There was absolute chaos as people jumped up and down shouting, ululating, whistling and generally having fun. John could only beckon to Priscilla to come to the stage, which she did. The crowd went into frenzy.

"Let him finish, let him finish!" shouted Pastor Baloyi over the hullabaloo. He had to repeat this over and over before people settled down to listen.

John went on.

"She…………………..," Again he did not finish for there was commotion at the front door. It looked as if someone was trying to get through. Actually, there were three people trying to come in. Pastor Baloyi shouted an order for them to be given room to pass. The three walked towards the stage, watched by an expectant audience. One of them was Michael and another Helen. It was the third person who caught John's attention. His smile broadened as his eyes focused on the boy at the head of the trio. He was carrying John's camera bag, but that was not what caught his attention. He knew that confident look and walk. He knew that skinny frame. He also knew that bright face. The boy was in different attire now. He was much smarter away from his cattle. It was him all right. The boy walked right up to John, stretched out his right arm so that he would shake his hand and started to speak.

"Hello, mister, and please pardon me for the interruption, my name is ...."

"Yeah, I know, Joe, Joe Sinyori. You were in the neighbourhood and when you heard the noise you came to investigate," said John, embracing the twelve-year-old boy who had done so much for him.

Everyone started clapping their hands although most were not quite sure about what the fuss was all about just yet.

ABOUT THE PUBLISHER

L.R. Price Publications is dedicated to publishing books by unknown authors.

We use a mixture of both traditional and modern publishing options to bring our authors' words to the wider world. We print, publish, distribute and market books in a variety of formats including paper and hard back, e-books, digital audio books and online.

If you're an author interested in getting your book published; or a book retailer interested in selling our books, please contact us.

www.lrpricepublications.com
L.R. Price Publications Ltd,
27 Old Gloucester Street,
London,
WC1N 3AX.
020 3051 9572
publishing@lrprice.com

www.ingramcontent.com/pod-product-compliance
Lightning Source LLC
LaVergne TN
LVHW010619100826
845148LV00014B/3038

* 9 7 8 1 8 3 8 0 6 1 0 5 0 *